marie claire
Maison
COLOUR

marie claire
Maison
COLOUR

Bridget Bodoano

First published in 2007 by
Quadrille Publishing Limited
Alhambra House,
27–31 Charing Cross Road,
London WC2H 0LS

Editorial director: **Jane O'Shea**
Creative director: **Helen Lewis**
Editor and project manager: **Anne McDowall**
Art direction and design: **Lucy Gowans**
Production: **Vincent Smith, Bridget Fish**

British Library Cataloguing-in-Publication Data
A catalogue record for this book is available from
the British Library.

ISBN: 978 184400 504 8

Printed in China

Contents

Colour is all around us in various forms. Nature gives us the brilliance of sky blue, grass green and poppy red but also the less definable, subtle colourings of a pink dawn, pebble greys and lichen greens. Away from the natural world, we are faced with a plethora of beautiful and varied colours in everything from clothing to building materials, and when it comes to interiors, the range of colours now available is huge, not only in paint, wallpaper and textiles, but also in flooring, furniture and accessories. Being presented with such a wide choice may be wonderful, but unless we have very definite ideas, choosing a paint colour for the walls can easily turn into a daunting rather than a pleasurable experience.

We all respond to colour in different ways, but our choice of colours for our home will be influenced by several factors, including not only our personal taste but also current fashions, the architectural style of our home and how we live in it. Colour has a huge impact on an interior and we can use it to

make a space feel cooler or warmer, larger or smaller, lighter or darker. But colour also has an effect on our emotions and we can use it to create an ambience to suit different moods. Bright colours are normally associated with energy and stimulation, while the paler, more neutral tones are thought to be more relaxing.

Just as there are fashions in clothes, interiors are subject to trends, and if you love the latest clothes, you probably also want your home to reflect your fashion credibility. But in the same way that the latest colours are not always the most flattering to our skin tones or hair colour, the latest vogue for interiors may not be the most suitable for you and your home. In addition, unlike with clothes, colour in the home is all around us, and most of us decorate to last for years rather than months – a good reason for any interior scheme to include a few timeless classics.

Your response to colour is a highly personal thing. Often the best and most interesting homes are those that reflect the personalities and passions of their owners, so don't be afraid to follow your instincts and give in to your emotions when it comes to choosing a colour scheme – it can have a direct effect on your wellbeing and will certainly make using colour in your home a more rewarding and enjoyable experience.

1
COLOUR EFFECTS

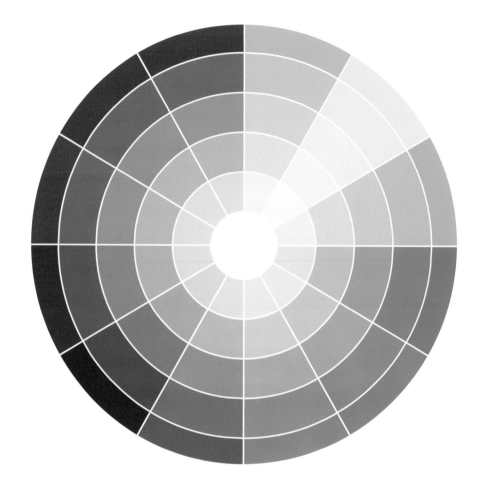

The Full Spectrum

Colour is a complex subject that has fascinated scientists and artists for many hundreds of years. While it is not necessary to fully understand the science of colour, it is useful to have an awareness of how colours are formed.

There are three pure or 'primary' colours: red, blue and yellow. Along with black and white, these colours can, in theory, be used to create all other colours. The strength and general appearance of colours will depend on many factors, including the source of the colour itself, the medium or material, and methods of manufacture. Over centuries, the introduction of new ingredients and techniques in the dyeing and printing processes has widened the scope of colour, and today's advances in science and material technology, including computer-generated images, means that many more variations, versions and intensities of colours are now available.

When exploring colour theory, it can be helpful to view colours within a colour wheel. Here you can see how the gradual adding of one primary to another changes red to orange to yellow, takes yellow through green to blue, and transforms blue into violet and then red. Colours containing red and yellow are generally accepted to be warm, while colours near blue are cooler.

Opposite: *This room appears as a joyful celebration of colour. The large space and pale-coloured walls and floor allow the very strong colours used for the furnishings, pictures and paper lanterns to make an impact.*

COLOURFUL LANGUAGE

The language used to describe colour is rich and varied and has occupied the pen and imagination of poets and writers for centuries. While there is a tendency toward the fanciful in the decorating business, the names given to colours can be useful, especially on colour charts, where a name can provide valuable clues as to the content, provenance, characteristics and mood of a particular colour. Descriptions may also include references to landscape, plants and wildlife as well as helpful words such as fresh, cool, calm or spicy. However, with so many colours now available, not all the names are perhaps quite so informative.

COLOURFUL TERMS

- **Hue** – colour
- **Tint** – colour with white added
- **Shade** – colour with black added
- **Tone** – colour with grey added
- **Monochromatic** – containing shades, tones and tints of only one colour
- **Achromatic** – no colour, just white, black and grey

These descriptions are not always used in their strictly correct manner, but it is generally accepted that 'shade' refers to variations of one colour and 'tones' to the strength or character. 'Tint' is commonly used to denote a small amount or hint of one colour in another.

The Effect of Colour

Colours vary according to their context and the quality and amount of light that falls on them, so it is not surprising that they, in turn, have an effect on their surroundings. Some of those effects are described here.

If there is one lesson to be learned about decorating with colour it is that you should always try out colours in a room before deciding on which one to use. Fortunately, these days many paint manufacturers sell trial sizes, which enable you to paint a large enough sample to be able to fully appreciate its impact. Wallpaper retailers will often cut a sizeable piece for you to try, and while shops may not be keen to supply a large sample of fabric, they will normally allow you to buy a small quantity. It really is worth spending some money on getting it right as mistakes can be expensive.

Colour on colour

Colours play tricks on the eye. The 'flicking' effect that occurs when you place bright red and bright green next to one another demonstrates how powerful the effect of one colour on another can be. Indeed, colours change depending on the colour they are next to. For example, orange on a red background will look yellow but orange on yellow will seem red. On green, it will appear as an even darker red but on violet it becomes more yellow. Colours will show up well against white, while on a black, indigo or purple background they can appear even more intense.

Taking the temperature

Reds and yellows tend to have a warming effect on an environment whereas blues and greens visually lower the temperature. The degree of warmth in a colour can be adjusted by mixing warm colours into cool ones and vice versa so that it is possible to have warm greens and blues and cool yellows. However, light and the other colours and materials used in a room can also visually warm or cool the atmosphere. Wood and textiles are good at warming while silvery metal and glass are effective coolants.

Sizing it up

Colour can have a dramatic affect on the size – or apparent size – of a room. On the whole, dark colours make a space feel smaller, while light colours will make it look larger, particularly if a single pale colour is used on everything, including walls, paintwork, floors and furnishings. A dark-coloured floor will make a room look smaller as will a brightly painted or papered wall or dark paintwork. Whether this matters and affects your choice of colour will depend on personal preference and the size of your space. Although the 'light and airy' feel is very much in vogue, a deep colour can be used even in a small room to make it feel warmer and more cosy, or just more fun.

Round the clock

Colours also change their appearance at different times of the day. This change can be quite dramatic and a colour that you love by day can become too warm, cold, dark or ineffectual in artificial light. For example, red looks darker at night whereas blue looks lighter. However, it can work the other way and colours that seem too heavy in the day can be dramatic and sexy at night.

Light show

White reflects light and black absorbs it, so it goes without saying that a

Right: *The power of colour to change the mood is well demonstrated here, where the same space appears in different guises from dark and mysterious through cool and energising to warm and sunny. The colours of the accessories have also been changed to enhance the effect.*

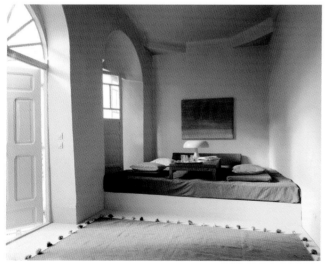

white room will feel and look bright and need less lighting than a dark one. However, the light-absorbing properties of colours are not always immediately obvious and some pale colours can be surprisingly difficult to illuminate. This is most noticeable with some paints and is partly due to the light-reacting properties of the constituents in the paint. This is particularly true of 'historical' paints, especially if they are manufactured according to traditional recipes, which not only contain more pigment but also have a grey base rather than the comparatively bright white base of modern paints.

Compass points

Rooms facing north or northeast generally appear cooler, and a colour that looks bright in a south- or southwest-facing room may look disappointingly dull in a sun-starved environment. For this reason, especially if you are using white, go for a warmer tone in cool rooms and keep the cooler shades for the sunny environments. And if you are using an intense colour in two rooms that face different directions, you may find you need to go one or even two shades darker to achieve the same effect in the north-facing space.

Seasonal effect

Just like the seasons, colours change their appearance throughout the year, and those that look fresh and bright in summer can turn cold and unfriendly in winter when harsher light, shorter days and lack of leaves change the ambience. This can be very noticeable in a room painted white, where the onset of colder weather may well change a fresh and bright room into one that is chilly and unwelcoming. In the same way, colours that warm up an interior during winter months may feel oppressive and too intrusive on hot sunny days.

Crossing continents

While travelling abroad, it is easy for us to be inspired by colours and to be tempted to try to incorporate them into our homes. However, colours that look good in one country may not work well in another where the light conditions and landscape are different. Deep, bright blue looks wonderful in Morocco or Greece but dark and forbidding in northern Europe. Terra cotta and creamy orange shades, which are great in Tuscany, take on a muddy hue in northerly climes. Conversely, pale yet subtle colours appear sophisticated in cool climates but suffer from the bleaching effect of bright sunlight.

Casting shadows

Different surface treatments and textures will also affect the appearance of colours. A smooth gloss paint will reflect light and therefore look lighter than the same shade in a matt finish. A flat piece of fabric will look darker when it is made up into curtains because the folds cast shadows, and similarly, a textured carpet can look darker when laid than it did in a small sample. Architectural features such as decorative mouldings and ceiling roses are subject to the same shadow effects, so if you want them to look the same colour as the walls and ceiling, paint them a shade lighter.

The Psychology
of Colour

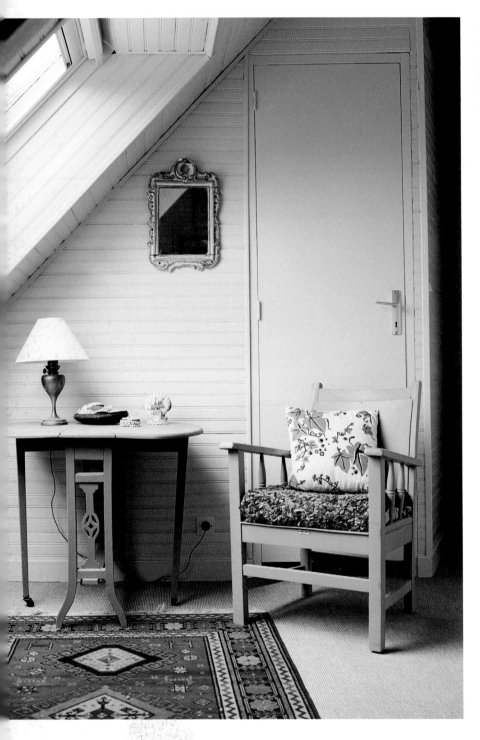

We all have our own response to colour: one person's gorgeous pink is another's sugary horror, and while some people think of red as energising and stimulating, others find it overpowering and even sinister. Many people believe that colour can exert a powerful psychological effect on our bodies and emotions and there is much evidence to back this up. Individuals often employ colour specialists to help choose clothes and interiors to suit their personality but professional colour consultants are also employed to ensure that public buildings, hospitals and offices provide an appropriate ambience, be it stimulating, soothing or even authoritative.

The psychology of colour is a fascinating topic but you don't need to study it in depth in order to find out what colours suit you. Trust your own instinct and don't be afraid to act on your initial response to a colour; after all, your brain and subconscious have a lifetime of research for you to draw on!

Although our response to colour is a very personal thing, however, there are certain generally accepted ideas regarding the character, effects and associations of different colours, some of which are shown opposite.

Left: *This green room, with chair and table painted to match the walls, looks clean, fresh and cheerful. The pretty printed cushions and rug add extra warmth and comfort.*

Red stimulating, hot, passionate, menacing, dangerous

Yellow warm, sunny, bright, happy, mellow, sickly

Blue cool, pure, clean, cold, melancholic, oppressive

Orange cheerful, warm, zingy, dominant

Green calm, natural, fresh, restorative, cold

Purple rich, sophisticated, spiritual, sombre, cheap

Pink soft, soothing, feminine, romantic, fun, sugary, sickly

Gold expensive, prestigious, mellow, decorative, brash

Silver cool, sharp, sophisticated, functional, cold

White pure, clean, light, cold

Black dramatic, elegant, sophisticated, depressing, sinister

Creating a Palette

We live in a fast-paced world and when we are decorating and improving our homes, we are often impatient to get it all done quickly. However, rushing the process sometimes leads to the wrong decisions being made on colours and furnishings and these mistakes can prove costly. It might be worth following the advice given in a book on interior decorating written in 1926: 'Never try to choose anything connected with the decoration of your house if you are tired. You must be able to concentrate and you cannot if you are fatigued. Don't try to choose too many things on one day as the senses become numbed and one loses one's judgment. Be lazy about it and slow in settling.'

INSPIRATION

If you find the idea of putting together a colour palette a daunting one, don't be shy about taking ideas from those who are very good at it. The palettes used by great artists and designers are freely available through postcards, books, magazines and exhibitions as well as shops, films and TV. If you like bright colours, take a look at the work of Matisse; if you prefer subtlety, look at the way colour was used in 18th-century houses; if you adore retro, study your favourite style in more detail; and if you are a fashion junkie, then take your colour lead from your favourite designers.

Don't rely simply on small samples of paint colours and fabrics – you will be unable to see how the colours react with one another. Colours look different against a white background, so when you are using paint charts, it's wise to cut out the colour swatch so that you can see how it works next to other colours. Try to use as large an area of colour as possible and make good use of trial-size pots of paint. Always take samples with you and try to make decisions at home – the lighting in shops makes colours look quite different from the way they will appear in a domestic environment.

When planning your colour scheme it is a good idea – and good fun – to gather together a collection of items containing not only colours swatches, textiles and flooring samples, but also postcards, fruit and vegetables, objects that will be in the room and favourite possessions – in fact anything that represents not only the colours but also the ambience you want to achieve.

PLANNING FOR COLOUR USE

When you are making decisions on colour, you will need to think about how the space will be used, by whom and when as well as taking into account the size and location of the room.

When do you use the room?
Wild colours and adventurous colour schemes may be great for a bathroom or small sitting room but for living areas in regular use it may be wise to tone things down a bit.

Who uses it?
If you share your home with others, don't forget to take their likes and dislikes into consideration.

What do you do in it?
Stimulating colours in a bedroom may keep you awake and in a sitting room may stop you from relaxing, but they could make you work better in a study and feel more cheerful slaving over a hot stove in the kitchen.

Opposite:
Paintings provide perfect palettes for an interior colour scheme. Here the colours of the wall and floor are taken directly from this wonderfully exuberant painting while still allowing it to be the centre of attention.

THE ART OF COLOUR SCHEMING

Here are a few painterly tips for you to consider before taking the final decisions on your colour palette.

- **Landscape**
  Take into consideration other colours around you – it may be the garden or view outside the window, or the colour of the walls in the neighbouring room.

- **Architecture**
  Take into account the style of the building – some colours suit some buildings better than others.

- **Portrait**
  Include a picture of yourself with all your samples – it sounds mad but you should be able to see if you look comfortable in your proposed colour scheme.

- **Still life**
  Take all your palette ingredients and make a still life in the room to be decorated so that you can see how everything reacts with each other in those particular surroundings.

- **Abstract**
  Don't confine yourself to paint and fabrics – a pair of striped woolly gloves or a bowl of blueberries and yogurt could be the basis for a colour scheme.

light

bright

brilliant

shine

snow

ice

WHITE LIGHT

crisp white cotton

freshly laundered linen

white chocolate

single cream

smooth white pebbles

It may be a cliché, but there's no denying that white makes things appear lighter and feel bigger, and for that reason it is an obvious decorating choice. If you are unsure what to do in your home and the old decor is hampering your thought processes, a coat of white will certainly clear the palette. Unfortunately, white is often seen as the easy option, a good solution when decisiveness and inspiration fail. But while plenty of white paint can undoubtedly be a panacea for the ills of a gloomy, tired interior, it really works best when it is a used as a definite statement. You should give as much thought to a white interior as you would to a more complex colour scheme.

A dark and dingy space can certainly be transformed with a lick of white paint into a much more pleasant environment, but white can also create an atmosphere that is cold, soul-less and uninviting. The success of a white interior depends on using the right white and your choice should take into account the quality of light and the architecture of your space as well as the colours and finishes on floors, fittings and furnishings. Nowadays there is a wide (and rather confusing) selection of whites to choose from. Many of the old 'historic' whites are not white at all but this still leaves plenty that are and they fall roughly into cool and warm categories depending on what other colours they contain.

Because of its ubiquity and low price, 'brilliant white' is a popular choice. However, it is not easy to use: this bright white contains blue and therefore tends to be cold and a little harsh. It is likely to sharpen objects and will highlight anything that is inferior in design or quality, or is grubby or damaged.

Often it is better to go for warm whites, which have very small amounts of red, yellow and brown added to create a gentler tone that softens edges, is kinder to furnishings and the eye, and creates a more restful ambience. Whites with a greenish tinge are known to be relaxing but they can look cold and clinical – more hospital than hospitable. However, some of the 'historic' whites contain more muted green undertones that are warmer and will work well in both old and new properties.

Opposite: *The use of white unifies the contrasting styles of the beautifully detailed panelling and the modern furniture in this room, creating an impression of simple elegance.*

White Out

The white box filled with white objects may have become a design cliché and therefore slightly unfashionable, but it can nevertheless look stunning, and for purist, disciplined minimalists, it is still the only colour of choice. Of course, you don't have to be a dedicated modernist or minimalist to make the all-white interior work well – though it does help if your virtues include tidiness and cleanliness. Few would disagree that white is perfect in spaces where the architecture is the main attraction because it will not detract from the design, but it can also be used in more prosaic surroundings where it will do the opposite and play down inadequacies, drawing attention away from unattractive features.

'White out' means not only white walls but also white furniture, fittings and accessories, white bedlinen, cushions and upholstery, lampshades, blinds, china, vases, bathroom fittings and tiles. If you want to go all the way, a white floor will complete the picture, increasing the feeling of light and space. In fact, a white floor is not as impractical as it sounds: white ceramic tiles, floor paint, vinyl or painted wooden boards are all hard-wearing, easy-to-clean surfaces, and unless you have pets and children providing a constant supply of footprints and spills, a white floor is easy to look after. Even if you think white would be impractical for large areas of floor, you could try it in a bathroom or small kitchen.

It is easy to get carried away with the all-white theme and you can end up spoiling the effect by over-accessorising. Try to resist the temptation to fill the space with white objects. You don't need to purify your home by throwing out anything coloured, just keep these things out of sight.

WAYS WITH WHITE

There are a number of ways in which you can use an all-white scheme, depending on the style of your home, your personal taste and the state of your bank balance.

Classy white out
This is the ultimate white experience, created with smooth, blemish-free surfaces, high-quality materials and finishes – think of white polished stone floors, modern minimalist furniture in acrylics and leather with shiny metal detailing. If a softer, more traditional style is your preference, however, you can opt instead for white painted bespoke wooden furniture and fittings with lots of white textiles.

Functional white-out
If your style aspirations exceed your surroundings and you lack the cash to bring it up to scratch, a covering of white paint will help to disguise shortcomings of furniture or surfaces and create a fashionable industrial or workshop feel. Rough walls, floorboards, old fittings, exposed brickwork and pipework all respond well to a coat of white.

Thrifty white out
If you tend to furnish your house from car boot sales and junk shops, why not try unifying everything with copious amounts of white paint and fabric. Paint walls, woodwork, floorboards, wooden shelves and fittings and furniture – even nasty stuff can look good under a generous coating of white eggshell or gloss paint – and dress the room with white curtains, blinds, bedlinen and lampshades to complete the look.

Economy white out

When it comes to buying inexpensive furniture, the safest colour choice is often white as the alternatives are usually veneers (which can look cheap and can be difficult to match up with other veneers), primary colours or colours that frankly look cheap. However, the variations in tone and character of white finishes can be a problem – buying everything from the same source can help.

Above: *Despite the uncompromising whiteness of this interior, it looks peaceful and cool rather than cold.*

Highlight

Even those who prefer a little colour in their lives will often opt for white in a bathroom or kitchen, where it is a natural choice for fittings, appliances and tiling. In functional rooms like these, in which the term 'clinical' is a compliment and not a criticism, white also looks business-like and efficient. Shiny surfaces are practical and normally easy to clean, though it is worth bearing in mind that they do show dirt and fingermarks and will therefore need regular maintenance.

The high-gloss, high-tech, high-spec look isn't confined to modern and minimal and doesn't preclude those with a taste for the old and traditional. Paintwork and floors covered with thick white gloss paint look wonderful in any situation, from a house with beautiful architectural details to a small cottage in need of brightening up. It's also a great way to add much-needed gloss to a featureless modern property.

SHINING EXAMPLES

Glazes
Use glazed tiles in bathrooms and kitchens. You can't go wrong with traditional square tiles, but look out for rectangular shapes, too. For a grown-up look, finish the edges with a moulded edging tile. Shiny tiles on a floor can be a safety hazard, but non-slip surfaces are available to enable you to complete the all-white look.

Glass and mirrors
Perfect shiny companions to white, mirrors reflect the glory of the white surroundings, and mirror tiles and white are a dazzling combination. Let white shine through glass, whether it's a glass shower cubicle or a glass-topped table.

Shiny metal
Sparkling chrome, stainless steel and aluminium keep white looking sharp. Complement the white with shiny fixtures, fittings, light fittings and appliances and take your pick from the wide range of lampshades, picture frames, storage containers, vases, bowls, bins and tableware. Though it is particularly effective in bathrooms and kitchens, shiny metal adds its sparkle to other areas and products, too, including furniture, not only as table and chair frames but also whole pieces such as chairs, stools, tables and cabinets.

Super-shiny finishes
Units with a high-gloss-painted or spray-painted finish give an aura of high quality to kitchen units and furniture, and several coats of high-gloss paint is a great way to rejuvenate floors and old furniture.

Acrylics
Smooth and classy, especially when used for curvy moulded furniture, acrylics can also be crisp and hard-edged for smart accessories and storage. Acrylic sheeting can be used for splashbacks or screens.

Right: *This wonderful glossy white floor turns an apparently ordinary space into something quite stunning and its impact is increased by the deliberately minimal style of the fittings and furnishings.*

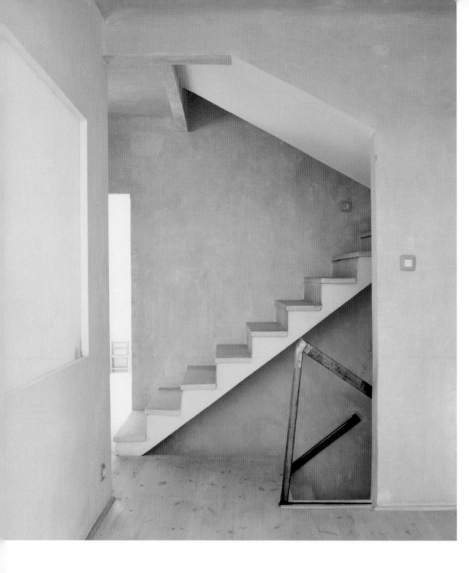

Lowlight

While it is true that white can look cold and unfriendly, it is possible to create a mainly white interior that is warm and even cosy – think creamy whites, the colour of white chocolate, vanilla ice-cream and undyed wool.

White can be warmed in several different ways. When it comes to paint, avoid brilliant white, which, with its touch of blue, is cool and unforgiving, and choose instead white with a hint of beige or warm yellow. (However, if your room has a sunny aspect, test these colours first as the cream could become too rich.) Some of the yellow tints added to white paint can be at the colder, greenish end and will create a

chill rather than warmth. There are plenty of warmer whites in the 'historic' ranges that use warm yellow ochre as a pigment and a base that is grey rather than dead white.

Warm whites tend to have a softening effect and can make a modern interior or a characterless space feel less intimidating. They are also more suitable in older properties where dead white feels too harsh. Sometimes a bright white, brightly lit interior is the right choice for a kitchen, bathroom or work space, but for more relaxing activities such as dining, a long bath or some quiet reading, you can calm things down by using softer lighting.

HOW TO WARM UP WHITE

• Choose warm white and cream shades for paints and textiles.

• Filter the natural light through warm-toned window coverings such as creamy gauze, unbleached linen or wooden slatted blinds.

• Use warm lighting – table lamps with warm-coloured paper, parchment or tinted glass shades.

• Accessorise with warm ochres, oranges, beiges and reds as well as plums and warm purples.

• Add firelight and candlelight for a comfortable warming glow.

• Team white with warm wooden floors, fixtures and fittings, furniture and accessories.

• Choose a 'soft' decorative style – old furniture, antiques and faded textiles have a mellowing effect.

• Literally add warmth in the form of woollen fabrics for upholstery throws, cushions and window coverings and carpet for floors.

Crisp and Even

When it comes to accessories, there is some truth in the saying that you can't go wrong with white, especially when buying inexpensive items, and this is certainly true of china, bedlinen, fabrics, curtains and blinds. Adding white accessories to a white interior will help to maintain the aura of order and cleanliness. Colour is not banned but introducing colour into a white room could spoil the atmosphere.

KEEP IT WHITE

Kitchen
Use white tea-towels, and make café curtains by clipping tea-towels on to a wire. Cover non-white table tops with white PVC-backed cloth or a cotton or linen tablecloth. Use white napkins and crockery and eschew stainless steel appliances and light fittings in favour of white. Not everything on open shelves has to be white – that would look too self-conscious – just make sure the shelves are white. If you do want to hide unattractive stuff, put it into white containers such as food storage jars, baskets and bowls.

Bedrooms
Opt for white bedlinen, bedcovers and cushions. Dress windows with white floaty voile, plain white linen or cotton curtains, white fabric blinds or smart, white metal slatted blinds. Keep to white light fittings and lampshades in fabric or paper. White baskets and boxes make attractive and unobtrusive storage.

Bathrooms
Use white fluffy towels and make sure flannels, shower curtains and bath mats are white, too. For windows, choose white blinds or make a simple curtain using a white cotton towel hung over a pole or clipped to a wire. Alternatively, you can't go wrong with white slatted blinds. Extend the white theme to fittings such as towel rails and light fittings including frosted glass. Finally, keep clutter under control in white painted wood, plastic or metal cupboards, shelves and drawers as well as plastic or basketware containers.

Living areas
Unlike white shoes, which are guaranteed to make your feet look huge, white upholstery looks less heavy as well as very chic. If, however, white is too impractical for you, opt for white throws and cushion covers in washable fabrics. As in a bedroom, you can maintain privacy and dress windows with white voile or, for a more formal look, choose lined curtains or Roman blinds made up in a heavier fabric. White roller blinds always look crisp and neat, as do white lampshades. White carpet is great for clean, well-behaved people but white (washable) rugs are a more practical alternative. If you want to be purist in your decoration, stick to white accessories – there are plenty of gorgeous white vases and objects to choose from.

Above: *This austere space with its hard surfaces is softened by the extensive use of white fabric for the curtains and throw. The white paper lampshades are the perfect choice as they create a soft form of lighting.*

Opposite: *The use of any soft furnishings other than a crisp, freshly ironed bedspread would have disturbed the tranquility of this beautifully simple bedroom.*

3

jeans and white t-shirt

blue and white china

black and white

Mondrian

WHITE PLUS

snowdrops

peppers and rice

strawberries and ice cream

bread and jam

Even if an all-white interior isn't for you, white still provides a good foundation for an uncomplicated colour scheme. White keeps things looking crisp and clean and can act as a unifying presence to tie in different colours throughout a whole house. Using it as the basis of an interior scheme also helps keep additional colour under control and prevents it from dominating. You don't have to stick to just one extra colour but it's best not to use more than two otherwise the look can get out of control. This is not as restrictive as it sounds because there are hundreds of shades within each colour to keep things interesting and lively.

One of the simplest ways to liven up an interior is to paint one wall of a white room in another colour. Picking out one area in paint or gorgeous wallpaper immediately changes the atmosphere and you can take things further by using shades and tones of the same colour in furniture, furnishings and accessories. When it comes to bright colours, pepper red, sunshine yellow, canteloupe and pistachio green look great in a kitchen, while crimson and violet will add sophistication to a sitting room. You can experiment with the more difficult aquamarines and turquoises in a dining room, hallway or bathroom. Choose a bright colour that suits your personality and that will have a positive affect on your mood, not just one that is fashionable – fabulous shades look great in the right place but that may be on a jumper rather than in your kitchen or sitting room.

If you prefer subtle to stark contrast, pick a softer colour for a gentler, less dramatic intervention. There are many wonderfully muted colours to choose from that might be too dark or sombre as an all-over look but that will add a touch of sophistication to what might otherwise be a rather mediocre scheme.

When choosing the 'plus' element, don't forget to take into consideration the colour of other features in the interior such as floor finishes, furnishings and fixtures and fittings. If these are dark or a definite colour then any added colour should be a variation on this theme – remember that too many plusses can add up to a minus! Whatever additional colour you choose, the impact will be more effective if you follow a few guidelines.

Opposite: *Beyond this room, the inky blue dining area has the air of a secret grotto while the dark tones of the stairs and wood panelling make them appear sculptural against the white walls.*

White Plus Red

White plus red is a potent combination and guaranteed to make quite an impact in any room. Red is cheerful and invigorating, responds well to light and works well by day and night – though it will look darker at night. What red you choose will depend on the context and your personal preference but because it is such a powerful colour, red needs to be used with care.

Bright, clear reds work well in a kitchen – think red peppers and tomatoes – but a deeper tone may be more restful in a sitting room. Red is not an obvious choice for a bedroom, where a calm atmosphere is conducive to sleep, but bedrooms are not always just for sleeping and a lively colour on one wall or a bedcover will relieve the coldness of an all-white environment. If you do choose to use red as a bedroom plus, you would be wise to put the red on the wall behind the bed so that it won't distract when you are trying to sleep.

INTRODUCING RED

Red's cheerfulness somehow stops it being oppressive but it is the colour with the longest wavelength and will appear to come 'forward' so bear this in mind when planning how and where to use it. You can lessen this forward effect by avoiding painting the wall that faces you on entering the room, or is facing you when you use the room – a sideways look may be less distracting and more restful. Red can make a small room feel smaller, while using a bright colour on the longest wall in a long, narrow room will make the space feel even narrower. Painting the shorter wall in a bright colour will help put things into proportion.

Painting one wall is a popular and easy way to introduce a bright colour but paint isn't the only way to add red: a red tiled splashback, floor, kitchen units or furniture are other options. If you opt for red units, they really need to be the star attraction and so will work better in a disciplined, uncluttered space where they can stand out against a pristine white background.

Blocks of colour work better than smaller bits and pieces, which is why red kitchen units work well, as would a large sofa, bed or rug. Smaller items of furniture create a more fragmented colour statement and therefore would benefit from being set off against a wall or floor of the same colour.

Red can look harsh, so add other colours to soften the impact. Golden yellows, oranges, purples and pinks work best and wood has a similar effect.

Above: *A glowing red box set into this kitchen turns washing up and cooking into a pleasure rather than a chore. The shelves provide a perfect backdrop for white china.*

Opposite: *In this living room, a curved wall has been painted in a brilliant glossy red. The dark floor and sofas create an air of sophistication, while the cushions provide extra colour and luxury.*

Above: *This colourful collection of accessories adheres to a strict colour code and therefore makes a bold statement against the all-white background.*

Below right: *The textured weave of the striped rug complements the stripped wood floor and provides a cheerful diversion from what could otherwise be an austere bedroom.*

Opposite: *Curtains and a textured wall help to soften this interior, while the red bedcover adds weight and colour.*

ACCESSORISE WITH RED

We all know how clever accessorising can brighten up a dull outfit or give a twist to something plain, and something as simple as a coloured scarf tied in a certain way can transform last year's fashion into this year's latest look. The style of an accessory can also dictate the look – a smart pair of shoes in this season's colour adds chic, while a length of brightly coloured ethnic cotton tied round the head or the waist looks more casual and more fun. The same applies to interiors, and using accessories as the plus in a white interior can work the same magic.

As with fashion, it is wise not to get carried away and over-do things – a pair of bright red shoes with an all-white outfit can look sensational but adding a red scarf, a hat and bag would look silly and would diminish the effect. Similarly, a single red rug can work wonders, as could a single stunning red vase, and this is because one block of colour or a playful splash makes more of an impact. In a kitchen, a row of red mugs looks great, but start dotting around red chopping boards, tea-towels, utensils, trays, storage jars and any more of the tempting array of coloured accessories that we find so hard to resist and it starts to look messy.

Think carefully about how and where you position these accent accessories. If you group a collection of red objects together on a set of shelves, for example, it will look clever and considered rather than messy. And while a single red rug might look lost on the floor, it could have a big impact hung on the wall.

Rugs and carpets

Lots of modern designs are bright and bold and they are sometimes surprisingly inexpensive. Look in junk shops and antique markets for old rugs, kelims and non-fitted carpets and keep an eye out for rag rugs. Oriental carpets go with anything and always look good, while kelims and dhurries are often cheap and cheerful and available in good colours.

Ceramics and glass

These are a good way to add splashes of colour, but don't go over the top – remember it's a home not a show house. If you favour a large collection, include a variety of shades and tones of one or two colours.

Cushions

Cushions provide an easy way to use bright colours and patterns, but again, don't overdo it. Keep the colours under control: it's much better to have three with the same or similar colouring plus one different than four distinct colours. And resist the temptation to cover everything in cushions, which not only looks messy but can actually make chairs and sofas quite uncomfortable.

Throws and bedcovers

The perfect opportunity for making a colour statement and one that allows you to experiment with colours you would be too afraid to commit to a wall. Throws and bedcovers provide a flexible way of adding colour that allows you to ring the changes seasonally.

White Plus Green

Green is a colour that we love to have around us in the form of trees and plants and it is generally accepted that green can have a beneficial effect on our wellbeing. Green is also associated with freshness – think of leafy glades or leafy vegetables – and nowadays the word green is also used to describe awareness of, and respect for, the environment.

You only have to look at a garden or landscape to realise how many shades of green there are. Green is created by mixing blue and yellow together, so it is obvious that those shades that contain more blue will be cooler and those with more yellow in them will appear warmer. Many shades of green also contain small amounts of red, which warms them up and prevents them from being too harsh.

Which green you choose will depend on your personal preference and where in your home you plan to use it, but green can be a difficult colour to get right because it changes its nature in different situations. Bright and dark greens can be particularly tricky as they can be cold, and the deeper shades used in any quantity can overwhelm. Green can make a room with small windows look gloomy, and at night, a bright green can change into something quite dark. It is also worth noting that green will cast its hue on everything around it – including people.

However, when used alongside plenty of white, green can look clean and crisp. For a stark contrast, the brighter greens are best used in places such as kitchens, while the darker shades can work well in a sitting room. As with any colour, particularly strong ones, it's a good idea to buy sample pots of different shades and try them out before making your final choice.

GREEN GAUGE

Grass
From the vibrancy of new spring grass to the gentler hues of summer meadows, this shade is great with white in kitchens, but it needs a sunny aspect – in a north-facing room it can feel very cold and looks darker. If you think of grass with flowers and blue sky you realise that any colour will go with it.

Lime
Lime is a bright and cheerful colour with dramatic tendencies and the right shade can work well in any room. However, it can lose its intensity in the absence of light or if it is too yellowy or has too much white or grey in it.

Forest
Dark green is a grown-up colour and can look very sophisticated in an elegant sitting room or dining room. It works best in spaces with high ceilings and plenty of light.

Olive
A more muted, yellowy green, which is warm and friendly. Olives can look dull without sunshine, though, and so will benefit from the addition of one or two other lively or clean colours. This is a good colour for living areas, especially as part of a retro scheme.

Blue-green
Blue-greens – from deep sea to emerald – can be cool and refreshing when in the presence of plenty of light and white and are therefore perfect for bathrooms. But they can also look wonderfully rich in a more traditional setting with antiques, luxurious fabrics, printed fabric and wallpaper.

WHITE PLUS GREEN PLUS ...

White and green on their own can sometimes look a little austere, but introducing a third colour will liven things up. There are many options:

- **Orange** – a tangy addition

- **Mustard** – from the hot yellow English to the milder French

- **Pale blue** – cleans and refreshes

- **Salmon** – the perfect accompaniment to lime and lettuce

- **Shocking pink** – livens things up

- **Rose pink** – a natural, and romantic, combination

Above: A bedhead provides a good opportunity to introduce a small but dramatic splash of bold colour into a room, especially when used with crisp white bedlinen.

MAKE IT WORK FOR YOU

White Plus Green Plus Red

Bold use of colour can change a perfectly nice white kitchen into something quite special. Bright colour works best if you apply it in one or possibly two designated areas so avoid the temptation to dot extra dabs of that colour elsewhere.

Green can be overwhelming when used in large expanses, but in a mainly white kitchen with white units it looks appropriately fresh and crisp. In this kitchen, the green panel above the sink appears lighter than the colour on the other wall owing to the light thrown on it from the side and without this light source alongside the sink, it is possible that the green above would have looked oppressive.

Green and white on their own can look a little cold and stark, which is why bringing in another strong colour, preferably something warm, is a good idea. Red and green together often have a dizzying effect on the eye that is anything but restful, but in this kitchen, where red has been added in the form of curvy acrylic furniture, the red is comfortably warm, and the reflective surface further softens the colour. If the floor had been white, the red and green would almost certainly have vied with one another for attention but here the dark floor calms things down.

Opposite: This kitchen looks pristine and functional, but with the addition of cheerful red furniture, it takes on a warm and friendly ambience.

COLOUR PALETTE

Lime green	Bright green	Red	Brown black	White
These yellowy greens add zest to any interior and, being lighter, work better than a grass green in a dark space. This paler green also works well with red.	*Clear, pure green looks fresh and clean but needs white to keep it bright. Like most bright colours, this green looks better in large blocks than in smaller areas.*	*This pure bright red, which looks as if it has come straight out of a paint tube, is warm and friendly as it leans toward yellow rather than blue.*	*Black is not only black: it contains other colours, which change its character accordingly. Brown-black is warmer and has a softening effect on the stark green, red and white.*	*Pure, bright, cool white is the right white to keep things looking clean and fresh. It is the shade most commonly used for smooth manmade materials found in kitchen fittings and appliances.*

ADDED INGREDIENTS

Stainless steel
Shiny and bright, it reflects the surrounding colours and keeps everything looking light. It sharpens up the white units and looks functional and efficient. Using it for the shelves and as a splashback keeps the number of different elements to a minimum.

Pictures
Placing a mainly white picture on the green wall adds light relief and stops the green from looking too heavy.

Furniture
This uncompromisingly modern furniture in wipe-down acrylic combines fun with functional, and opting for stools rather than chairs keeps things looking neat.

Floor
The shiny surface of this floor echoes the rest of the furniture and fittings, but a wooden or tiled floor would work just as well. Choose a dark colour to help ground a brightly coloured room.

White Plus Blue

Anyone who has travelled to hot, sunny countries such as Greece cannot fail to be enchanted by the simple vernacular architecture, much of which is painted pristine white with details picked out in deep blue.

In Mediterranean countries, blue helps to bring the temperature down, but in more northerly climes, it can be a cold, hard colour. Nevertheless, blue is a natural companion for white, whether it is adding a dash of authority to a uniform or gentle prettiness to a china teacup.

Pure blues include Prussian blue, ultramarine, lapis lazuli and the softer indigo, but in the colour wheel blue goes from the deepest blue green to darkest purple and it is a main component in a wide palette ranging from turquoise to lavender. Dark or bright pure blues can be chilly, but the greyer blues, such as those found in traditional paints, can be wonderfully warm, and because blue 'recedes', you can get away with slightly darker shades in a small room.

BLUE MOODS

Blue and white is a classic colour combination that can be found in many guises, including favourite outfits and everyday objects, and can form the basis of a variety of different decorating styles.

Denim and white
Think how timeless the jeans and white shirt look is: it never goes out of fashion, looks good in almost any situation and always feels comfortable. Denim is strong and hard-wearing and great for upholstery, throws, cushion covers and curtains. And if you are handy with a needle, why not make throws and bedcovers (line them with fleece for extra warmth) and big bags for linen or for storing clothes, toys, sewing, spare bedlinen and anything else that needs a place to hide?

Blue and white stripes
From the bold blue of butchers' stripes to the neatness of ticking, blue and white stripes are ideal for upholstery, cushions, curtains and blinds. Roman blinds made from crisp white ticking with a narrow blue stripe add just enough blue to sharpen up a white room. It's easy to find blue and white stripes in a variety of fabrics – and don't forget checks and spots either.

Blue and white china
For a feminine touch, take inspiration from Delft, willow pattern, country scenes, pretty florals on porcelain and functional chunky deep-blue glazed pots and jugs. The deep intense blue used for decoration on ceramics is provided by the use of cobalt, which contrasts beautifully with the white background. For a smart, sophisticated look in a bathroom, top off white tiles with a narrow border of dark blue edging tiles.

Lavender and lace
Pretty, romantic, nostalgic; call it what you will, a white room dressed in pretty lavender blue and white florals, some toiles de Jouy and a little lace is irresistably charming and a look that is not difficult to achieve.

Abstract expression
If you are into art and modernism, why not paint a wall in Yves Klein blue? This dense but brilliant colour will make a huge impact, which is the whole point.

Opposite, top: The soft indigo blue of the cushions and bedlinen adds a touch of warmth and softness that is very appropriate for a sleeping area, especially one as simple and basic as this one.

Opposite, bottom: The neatness of this cool sanctuary is emphasised by the adherence to a strict blue and white colour scheme. The stark contrast provided by the blue-painted window frames is softened by the pale blue used in the decorative border and painted stools.

White and Dark

A very dark colour added to a mostly white interior is bound to have great impact, especially when used over an extensive area such as a wall, ceiling or floor. This dramatic effect is often used by architects and designers in large, modern interiors to manipulate the space. A dark ceiling will appear lower and a dark floor makes a space feel smaller, both useful devices for making big spaces feel more human in scale. Deep-coloured walls have a similar effect. Think carefully before using dark colours in a small room, where the result can be claustrophobic.

As with most bold uses of colour, discipline is required, a small palette is essential and a pared-down, uncluttered environment the recommended style. There are many ways to introduce a dark element into an interior scheme, including paint, dark wood and fabrics. Good paint colours include dark browns, battleship greys and midnight blues, plus all the different versions of black from steely blue-black to dramatic purple-black.

A white and dark theme is perfect for modern, pared-down interiors but it can also look elegant and sophisticated in older houses and with old and antique furnishings. As with bright colours, it is important to use a dark colour in blocks; small amounts will not work effectively. A dark wall is a perfect backdrop for beautiful furniture of any style while a white room looks wonderful with slabs of dark, sleek modern furniture and upholstery, especially if they're placed on a white floor. Dark curtains and blinds can look bleak against a blank white wall and therefore should not be used as the only dark element in a room. They will work much better if the floor and some of the furnishings are also dark.

When using dark colours, it is important to get the right balance of light and dark in the interior as a whole. Dark is heavy, so keeping dark colours to the lower part of a room, leaving plenty of white above, will keep things looking light. A dark floor on its own in a white space can look a bit lost, so give it a purpose by including it as part of a scheme that features other dark elements such as furniture and fittings.

Dark colours can be difficult to spend a lot of time with, which is why a bathroom is a good place to try them out; the plain shapes of fittings will look good against a dark background. Dark base units in a kitchen can look great, but dark wall-cupboards could be too overpowering, so either confine cupboards to one wall or, if you have high ceilings, leave a space between the top of the cupboards and the ceiling. A white floor could also help to maintain balance.

When it comes to finishes, matt emulsion and wool, linen and thick cotton upholstery fabrics look chic but so, too, do glossy surfaces, and these will also reflect the light.

Right: *This minimal kitchen has obviously been designed to be functional, yet it is also beautiful. Nothing is allowed to detract from the impact of a slab of dark colour set in a white environment. The concealed lighting prevents it looking too austere.*

Above: *The walls of this bathroom have been painted a similar dark colour to the counter top. Keeping to white accessories makes everything look crisp and fresh.*

Opposite: *The warmth of the dark, well-worn wooden floor prevents this resolutely minimal interior from looking too cold and clinical. It also provides a contrasting texture to the smooth finishes of the furniture and paintwork.*

DARK MATERIALS

Our obsession with the light and airy means that we often neglect or dismiss dark materials as too heavy, which is a shame – those such as dark woods and stone have wonderful qualities as well as beautifully subtle colouring.

Wood
Dark wood has an essentially warm feel, which is why it works so well in a modern, pared-down interior. There is a huge variety of solid woods and veneers available, with colours ranging from almost black to deep nut browns. The natural graining in wood provides texture as well as surface interest and prevents even very dark wood from looking too heavy. In both old houses and more prosaic homes, dark wood floors and furniture provide character as well as warmth, and wood has a mellowing effect on stark white paint. A dark wood floor can make a room look small but dark wood furniture, whether modern or antique, stands out beautifully against a white background. Many contemporary interiors feature dark wood panelling, which looks smart and sophisticated when used in moderation with plenty of white.

Stone and composites
Stone is increasingly being used in interiors and in more adventurous ways, and dark stone has a distinctive, solid and practical presence that adds weight as well as contrast to a mainly white interior. Granites, slates and marbles can be found in a subtle range of colours, including black, grey, dark greens and deep reds, and in a choice of polished, matt and textured finishes. There are also several composites and ceramics that look like stone, some of which are cheaper and more practical than the real thing. As well as fireplaces, worktops, splashbacks and surrounds, it is also possible to get basins, sinks and baths that are made out of stone or stone-like materials. Stone is available in large sheets or cut or moulded forms as well as tiles.

Paint
Unless we are painting a front door or the garden gate, we seldom explore the darker end of the paint charts, fearing that such colours would be just too overpowering in a domestic interior. While it is true that very deep colours should be used with caution as they absorb light, bring walls in and ceilings down, they also lend dramatic relief to a bland white space. Dark browns, greys and even black can look chic and very sophisticated, but these colours do work better in a simple, sparsely furnished interior. Go for cool browns that have a touch of grey, and greys that are slightly warm. If you are brave enough to use black, you will find quite a selection, from warm browny black to steely blue-black and those with a greeny tinge.

Paint comes in several different finishes. A gloss-painted dark wall will

make a very bold statement and the fact that it reflects light can make it appear less dark, but a matt finish gives a more subtle effect.

Wallpaper

A bold wallpaper can make quite an impact on a room and whereas a painted wall is a solid block of colour, a patterned paper is less heavy. While dark wallpaper may be too much for a whole room, it can look fabulous as the dark interest on one wall of a white room. Look for damask patterns on dark backgrounds and retro sixties patterns with lots of dark browns and greens. The deep blues and greens in dark William Morris prints still look great even in a modern setting, and now that wallpaper is hot once more, there are plenty of fantastic new options to choose from.

Textiles

Dark-coloured upholstery, carpets, rugs, curtains and blinds add substance to a white room, but smaller items look better if they are grouped together to form a solid block of colour rather than used in isolation. Dark carpets can look great when newly vacuumed, but they do show the bits; dark woollen rugs, either plain or patterned, are generally more practical. For upholstery and window coverings, look for smooth plain wools and tweeds in browns and greys, or for a more glamorous or traditional look, choose velvets and damasks. Plains are good, but dark patterns provide extra interest and relief to lighten the atmosphere.

Metal

Instead of shiny, go for dark, painted metal and enamelled finishes such as those used on range cookers and metal funiture. Wrought iron is naturally dark and rustic, and ethnic metal furniture and accessories have a dark patina that stands out beautifully in a white interior.

Left: *The dark wooden floor and imposing leather sofa add extra luxury to this classy bathroom, as do the carefully positioned shelves and their contents.*

Below left: *The stark simplicity of the white sofa stands out beautifully against the dark wall. The patterned rug and striped lampshade bring in other dark touches.*

Opposite: *In another situation, dark structural beams together with dark upholstery could look very heavy. Here, however, the huge windows and white floor prevent these dark areas from looking oppressive. Instead, they complement and emphasise the architecture.*

Subtle Contrast

Sometimes painting everything white is the easiest and most successful way in which to bring a sense of order to a home. White can disguise inadequacies, lighten dark spaces, enlarge small ones and discipline awkward ones, and it is also good for unifying an otherwise disorderly interior or collection of items. But if you want a little relief from white and prefer subtle rather than stark contrast, there are various ways to do it.

Maintaining an aura of calm is a priority and therefore any deviation from white needs to blend in rather than stand out. Remember that colour doesn't necessarily have to be in the form of paint or fabric: materials such as wood and stone also have colour and can play their role. Adding a few gentle-toned fabrics, coloured walls or a wooden floor to a white interior will make it feel less austere without losing the sense of space.

SUBTLE DISTINCTIONS

Wood
A wooden floor is the perfect way to soften an all-white space, but for subtlety, choose the lighter colours and finishes. If you are stripping the floors, finish them with a clear varnish or oil, and think about treating doors, window frames and any wooden panelling in the same way. Make light-coloured wood the material of choice for floors, shelving, furniture and kitchen units as well as fixtures, fittings and accessories.

Wallpaper
Pale-coloured prints on white backgrounds are ideal for prettying up a bedroom and you could use bolder designs in subtle colours on a single wall in a living area or hallway.

Painted surfaces
Use subtle colours such as darker 'old' whites, creams, pale greys, beiges, blues and greens on walls, woodwork, floors and furniture. In a white kitchen, pale green or blue units look fresh and clean. In a bathroom, pale green tiles look relaxing and smart.

Softeners
Fabrics, cushions, throws, curtains, blinds, wall-hangings, carpets and rugs make things feel as well as look softer. Natural and unbleached cottons and linens and undyed wools are great for warming up white, and the different shades and tones of natural fabrics and fibres work together to create harmony. If bare floors are too hard or noisy, natural-fibre floor coverings such as sea grass and sisal are a good alternative. When it comes to coloured textiles, natural fibres take dye in such a way as to give a deeper, more subtle colour.

Below left: *Using accessories in different textures and materials is a good way to introduce subtle contrast within a very small colour range.*

Opposite: *Apart from the bath, all the elements in this bathroom share a similar tonal quality. The mirror, though dramatic, provides subtle contrast in the form of reflected colour.*

Splash it About

Adding colour to white doesn't necessarily require restraint, but you will need to exercise a little self-discipline with larger splashes of colour to prevent things getting out of hand. Confining the colour to a single area, level or plane will ensure maximum impact. Even a joyful riot of colourful furniture can be tamed if the height of the various pieces – particularly seat-back height – is roughly the same, and if other colourful distractions are not allowed to stray above that line. A dark or similarly coloured floor will also help to hold the colour down in its defined area and give a more cohesive result.

SPLASH, DON'T SPLATTER

Avoid the temptation to dot small bits of colour around, which will result in an unfocused, bitty look. The important thing is to keep control and to use colour in large areas such as upholstery, pieces of furniture, rugs and perhaps some pictures. It also helps if you obey the rule of limiting the palette to one or two strong colours plus shades and tones of those colours. When choosing your colours, don't forget to take into consideration other colour elements in the room such as furniture, fittings and the floor.

Opposite: *This unusual artwork was clearly the source of the deceptively disciplined colour scheme here – the colours of all the various accessories are to be found in the painting.*

FAMILY TIES

Confining yourself to even just one strong colour still allows plenty of scope for colourful compositions. Consider some of the other colours tied to these primaries, for example:

Bright yellow – egg-yolk yellow, mustard, pale yellow, lemon, lime, orange, burnt orange.

Bright red – deep red, maroon, pinks, red-purple, mauves.

Bright blue – dark blues, pale blues, turquoise, blue-greens, blue-greys, blue-purple.

Bright green – forest green, blue-greens, pale greens, lime, grey-greens.

CHEAP AND CHEERFUL

Sometimes the simplest things give the most pleasure for least amount of effort. It's easy and fun to cheer up a plain white interior with a pot of paint and a few colourful accessories. Choose a small but cheerful palette of colours that includes one paint colour and a collection of fabrics containing either that colour or contrasting ones in similar tones.

Painting furniture is an easy way to add colour: paint a single chair, a chest of drawers, a mirror or a large picture frame or collection of small ones. Junk shop finds are perfect for this sort of makeover but cheap new equivalents can be given a fresh personality with a coat of paint. Complete the splash of colour with a collection of cushions and perhaps one or two accessories such as a basket or small table. This approach is good in bathrooms, kitchens and bedrooms where a more relaxed look is more appropriate. In a living room, you can make bigger splashes with a bigger mirror, pictures, a sofa and cushions, and perhaps a rug.

MODERN MANNERS

When the Modernists designed their simple, elegant furniture (much of which is still available today), they also developed a fashion for painting rooms white. But in fact the Modernists did have colour in their homes and they placed their designs among beautiful – and colourful – objects and artworks. Today, architects, designers and lovers of all things modern often favour the stark white, minimalist box in which to display their treasures. However, your surroundings say much about you, and if you're not careful, an all-white interior could give the impression that you are either unimaginative or frightened to show your real personality.

Left: *This bathroom has been cheered up with summertime colours, including limey and grass greens, warm sunny yellow and some hot pink stripes and checks.*

Below left: *The coloured chairs and table top are allowed to be the centre of attraction in this understated environment – even the carefully arranged objects are uniformly muted.*

Above: *White is the perfect choice as a backdrop to this collection of mostly modern furniture, pictures and objects, but the wooden floor and shelving help create an overall impression of warmth and comfort.*

Modern furniture can look very severe and unwelcoming in a white space so it will benefit from the company of a few of your favourite things. The perfect way to display a collection of pictures or objects is on shelves and it works best if you restrict shelving to one wall or section of wall and treat that area as an art installation. Paintings look great if they are propped up on a narrow shelf rather than hung on the wall. A collection of pictures gathered together in one area looks more interesting than dotting them

around the room and allows you to change the displays frequently without making holes in the wall. It also enables you to keep the other walls free of pictures in modern, minimalist fashion. You don't have to follow a colour theme – if pictures are good they will work well together no matter what their subject or colouring – though if you want to play the coordination game, that's fine. You can also use the colours in the pictures or objects as a palette for cushions and throws, but remember to keep it simple.

MAKE IT WORK FOR YOU

Splash it About

Confined to one end of an otherwise all-white space, what appears as an extremely exuberant burst of colour is in fact quite disciplined. The vibrant pink takes centre stage: it can't be ignored and so the other colours have been carefully chosen so as not to compete for attention. A relatively small area of hot pink is on show – any more and it would be overpowering – and if it wasn't for the unconventional patchwork quilt with its dark reds, purply browns and acid greens, it would take over completely. Although the pink is undoubtedly bright and the whole picture makes a real splash, the colours of the other cushions are in fact quite restrained. The amethyst is a slightly pinky version of purple, similar in tone to the lighter pink, which means that they harmonise rather than shout.

The reason this scheme works so well and looks so dramatic is that it is confined to a relatively small area. Use of the brightest colour is restricted and the patchwork cover made up of squares of several colours work better than one slab of colour. The rest of the space is uncompromisingly white and the temptation to take the colour theme elsewhere has been resisted. A coloured lampshade, a pink rug or bright curtains would have spoiled the effect completely. The picture is the only other source of colour but positioned above the divan it is part of the whole scene rather than a distraction.

Opposite: Despite the stark whiteness of its surroudings, this colourful niche looks both cheerful and inviting – the perfect place for a quiet read or a cosy chat.

COLOUR PALETTE

Vivid pink	**Pale pink**	**Amethyst**	**Pale lime**	**Chocolate brown**
A loud colour that demands attention and certainly gets it in a white setting. It requires careful handling and is best used in controlled amounts.	*Adding white to vivid pink could be a bit sugary so choose a subtler version that calms it down with a touch of grey.*	*Hovering between purple, pink and blue, this is the perfect colour to tone down the excesses of bright pinks or purples.*	*Lime green offers a refreshing antidote to pink, but with vivid pink, a paler lime is best – it will complement it rather than trying to compete.*	*Used in small quantities, the rich tones of chocolate add warmth and weight, preventing pink from being too overpowering.*

Shock Tactics

The great fashion commentator Diana Vreeland famously called shocking pink the navy blue of India, and wearing it – or using it in your home – does require a certain amount of good fashion sense. Like navy blue, shocking pink is perfect with white, but unlike navy, which can form the basis of an outfit, bright pink is more of an accessory colour to be used with flair and confidence. For interiors, shocking takes the girly out of pink: it is still feminine but more strong woman than dizzy blonde and more chic than chick, though hippy can be hip.

Pink can be a bit much on walls, so use it as you would with clothes – a jacket, shirt or scarf, but not the whole outfit. One of the best places to use shocking pink is on upholstery. Thick cottons, linens and wool give depth to the colour, and used on a sofa, armchair or a bedhead it makes a good solid splash against a white background.

As shocking pink is such a dominant colour, the no-clutter rule is best obeyed, but if you do want to add other colours, go for refreshment in the form of lime greens, acid yellows and even a dash of turquoise, or take a more subtle approach with amethyst, purple and paler pinks. Pink in a white interior, especially if the floor is white too, certainly can't be ignored, but it can look more grown-up and sophisticated on a dark floor.

IN THE PINK

Pink chic
Maintain your composure in elegant surroundings with just the right amount of pink to show your wilder side. Keep it smart with smooth fabrics, clean lines and disciplined simplicity. Make pink and white sophisticated by teaming it with dark wood, stainless steel and chrome and a few well-chosen white accessories.

Pink hippy
Connect with your inner hippy and kick against the anti-clutter brigade with a comfy casual look. Pick out the shocking pink with floaty voile at the window or even round a bed, kelims and dhurries, ethnic objects, baskets and jolly plastics. Keep the pink dominance in check with flashes of turquoise, lime greens and amethyst.

Pink glamour

Glam it up and embellish your white interior with luxury fabrics – think pink velvets, silks, satins and damask – a few ornate objects and a touch of gold. If you are feeling adventurous, you can add a wall of pink patterned wallpaper or, if you really want to shock, over-long, heavy, silk damask curtains hung from a gilded pole. Add one or two elaborate pieces of furniture and accessorise with gilded picture frames and mirrors, pretty lamps and perhaps a chandelier.

Opposite: *The dark floor and modern furniture has a sobering effect on the pink sofa, making it appear smart and sophisticated rather than frivolous.*

Above: *The use of pink for the sofa, table and delightfully quirky sculpture in an otherwise all-white room adds a touch of femininity and glamour.*

primary colours

rainbows

paintbox

colouring crayons

shocking

electric

GLORIOUS
TECHNICOLOUR

startling

luminous

riot of colour

Matisse

Monet

Kandinsky

If you love bright colours and like to surround yourself with them, don't be afraid to use them in your home. A vividly coloured interior is not exactly relaxing, but it doesn't have to exhausting either, and there are things you can do to prevent your colour wheel from spinning out of control.

If you are not sure how you want to colour your particular world, take your inspiration from art. Look at the glorious colours in the paintings of Kandinsky, for example, or note Van Gogh's famous yellow chair and bed and the colourful, sunny California as painted by David Hockney. A postcard of a painting by a favourite artist provides a ready-made palette for a colour scheme and is likely to be far more subtle and sophisticated than anything you could come up with on your own. You may also be surprised to find that the number of colours used is more restricted than you imagined and that many of the colours are more muted than they appear.

Colours react with one another in unexpected ways and play tricks on our eyes and brains. Placing colours next to one another often has surprising consequences with bright colours losing their intensity and apparently dull colours springing into life. A shiny colour will look lighter than a matt finish while textures throw shadows and make colours appear darker. When using a colourful palette, the influence of light, position and orientation of a room become even more pronounced and therefore it is very important to try out colours in their intended setting before committing to them.

The large numbers of paint colours, wallpapers and textiles on offer is wide and wonderful, but if you are daunted by so much choice, try restricting your palette to products from a specific company, manufacturer, designer or shop as they are likely to all share similar characteristics of tone, style and basic materials, which means that they will naturally work together.

Opposite: Such a wonderfully bold use of colour is the perfect way to make a feature of an area in the home that is often not given the attention it deserves.

Primary School

In theory, any colour can be made by mixing different amounts of red, blue and yellow, which are known as primary colours. When it comes to interiors, don't get too hung up on the correct definition of 'primary' – the term is often used to describe all the strong, bright colours, including green, violet and orange, that are found in the rainbow. In their undiluted state, the characteristics of these colours will be reinforced. Red appears to come forwards and blue recedes, and red, yellow, orange and purple feel warm, while blue and green are cooler.

The strength of these colours means that they have a powerful effect on one another and they will vie with each other for attention. It is therefore advisable not to use too many in one area. Instead, include variations of the colours in the form of tints, tones and shades, colours produced by adding white, grey and black respectively.

Using strong colours takes nerve and some talent, so don't be afraid to enlist the help of people who know how to handle their colour. For example, look at the paintings of Matisse, which are full of pure bright colours but also contain some wonderfully subtle ones that play an important role in the balance and composition. Include some of these in your palette to help you to create your own interior compositions.

Using primary colours with white (see chapter 3, White Plus) is perhaps the safest and easiest option, but for a more intense experience, be bold and use them as the main attraction and in larger quantities. Though bright colours are often associated with all things modern, colour schemes of the past were often much more colourful and adventurous than those of more recent

times: whole rooms in deep blues, reds and greens were a feature of stately homes as well as more modest houses. Today, many older properties are given a coat of white to make them look 'modern' when in fact they would be more comfortable in colourful clothing. Similarly, bright colours add personality to new or more prosaic homes. Be brave: impress your friends (and yourself) with a sapphire blue or sunny yellow dining room, a bright red sitting room, a cobalt-blue bathroom, a purple bedroom or a lime-green kitchen.

Studying the theory of colour is one way of understanding how colours work with each other but it is a complex subject and is not necessarily the ideal way to discover what works best in a north-facing bedroom, for example. Choosing how to decorate your home is a combination of personal taste, natural instinct and experience, and there is a lot to be said for doing your own thing rather than following the orders of strict interior advisers, especially as colour – and our response to it – is a very personal thing. Nevertheless, a few facts and guidelines can be helpful.

Opposite: *A neutral background allows bright colours to shine. Here, the bright green and red stand out beautifully as they have nothing else to compete with.*

Below: *The use of red and black makes this a very dramatic interior redolent of old castles or palaces. The minimal furnishings help to maintain a feeling of space despite the dark colours.*

PAINTING CLASS

Faced with a paintbox of bright colours it is easy to get carried away and end up with a mess rather than a work of art. Following a few guidelines will help to ensure that your colourful ideas become successful colour schemes.

● Don't use too many colours – the trick is to add interest in the form of tints, tones and shades of one or two colours rather than a different primary.

● For a more restrained look, paint the walls in subtle or neutral shades and introduce bold colour in the form of upholstery, rugs, curtains, blinds and accessories – but don't use too many different colours or it will look bitty.

● Painting floors and furniture in bright primaries is a great way to add colour as well as an economical way to make the most of what you've got.

● Avoid the temptation to populate brightly coloured upholstery with a rainbow of coloured cushions. It will look smarter with a collection of cushions in the same colour or variations of that colour, plus perhaps one bright contrast.

● If a bright colour on every wall is too much, paint one wall bright and do the rest in a paler shade or tint or another subtle colour.

● White makes colours look more intense and can create too much contrast. Brilliant colours will look more sophisticated when set against subtle colours such as beige and warm grey, and will respond well to the mellowing effects of wood floors and furniture.

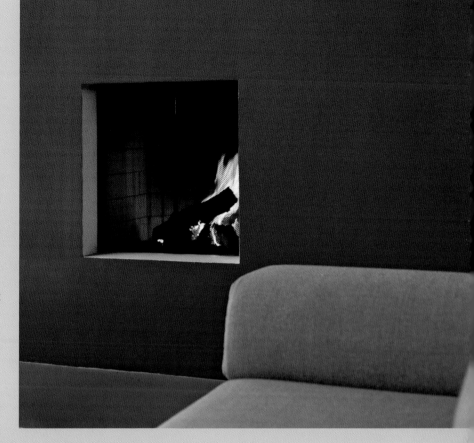

● Instead of adding another colour, use varieties of one colour in the form of different textures and finishes. Add interest with gloss, eggshell and matt paint, chunky and smooth textiles in rugs and upholstery, textured wall-coverings and coloured furniture and accessories in a variety of materials, from smooth glass, metal and plastics to rougher painted wood and baskets.

● Add pizzazz with brightly coloured prints and patterns in the form of fabrics and wallpaper. Set them against a plain shade chosen from the colours contained in the pattern.

Above: *Blue and red can be difficult together, but here the brilliance of the kingfisher blue works beautifully against the earthy red.*

Opposite: *Shades of red are not an obvious choice for a bathroom but perhaps these wonderful old tiles were the inspiration. The pristine whiteness of the bath shines out against its dark surroundings.*

RED

- Primary attraction: yellow, orange and purple

- Bright contrasts: bright pinks, brilliant blue

- Calming effects: pale pinks and mauves, brown, dark grey, deep purple

YELLOW

- Primary attraction: red, blue, purple, orange

- Bright contrasts: brilliant blue, violet

- Calming effects: pale blue, indigo, taupe, brown

BLUE

- Primary attraction: red, yellow, orange

- Bright contrasts: bright pink, lime green

- Calming effects: pink, mauve, brown, olive green, mustard

GREEN

- Primary attraction: yellow, red

- Bright contrasts: bright pink, light blue, bright mustard

- Calming effects: taupe, dark brown, deep purple

RED AND YELLOW

Reds and yellows are at the warm end of the colour spectrum and therefore are a good way to bring cheer into your home. However, the strong presence of these colours can prove too overbearing if you are not careful.

Yellow is, on the whole, a happy colour associated with sunshine, and it can indeed brighten up a dull or gloomy space. Intense yellows, such as egg-yolk, veer toward orange and are therefore undoubtedly warm, but the more greeny yellows, such as lemon, can be surprisingly cool. Similarly, reds containing yellow are warm and soft whereas those containing a lot of blue are cooler and can look harsh.

Red is a popular and ubiquitous colour. Most product ranges – whether of ceramics, fabrics or furniture – will offer a choice of red. It also regularly crops up in patterns, where in combination with other colours, it adds depth, definition and interest. Red works well with most colours but also looks good on its own. As paint or wallpaper, it can have a very grand appearance in a room with high ceilings and traditional or antique furniture, but it is also a good colour for an intimate, cosy sitting room. However, bear in mind that, as red looks darker at night, a colour that appears bright and cheerful in daylight could turn heavy and sinister in artificial light.

Yellow can look good almost anywhere, but an all-over, bright yellow experience can be too overpowering in a small room unless there are large windows and plenty of light. It is a softer option than red and is good for cheering up hallways and kitchens – and children love it in their bedrooms and playrooms. It is a mistake to think of yellow only in cheerful, sunny terms, however, as it can look wonderfully sophisticated and elegant in a high-ceilinged dining room or bedroom.

Opposite: *This brilliant red and yellow bathroom with its mirror-tiled floor is quite outrageous and would certainly wake you up and buck you up. Such a colour scheme could be overwhelming, but as a bathroom is used for only short periods of time, it is a good place to be adventurous.*

Vivid Scenes

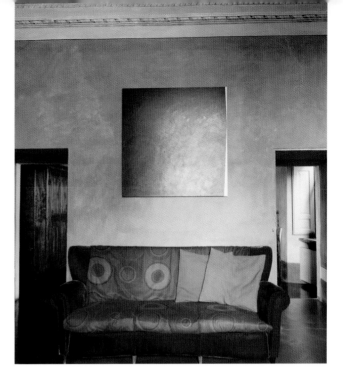

Beautiful old houses deserve respect, but they don't have to remain trapped in the past. For some, not sticking to an historically correct colour scheme may be seen as shocking and insensitive, but in fact the colour schemes of the past were often much more colourful and exuberant than we, admiring of peeling paint and faded glories, realise. An over-the-top fantasy palette is not an easy thing to get right, but if you love that sort of thing, and think you could live with it, it's worth a try. You don't have to live in an architectural gem to get this style to work successfully, but you will have to moderate your colours and modify the look to suit a smaller space.

STRONG HINTS

Choose colours of similar intensity
Choosing colours with the same strength and characteristics is made easier with helpful paint colour charts where the colours are divided into 'families' and 'moods', often with further categories based on how the colours are made up. Picking all the colours from one specific category ensures a consistent look. Some of the 'historic' colour charts are not divided in this way, but their colours already share quite a strong character, and as they normally contain more pigment, the strong colours are naturally intense.

Buy everything from one supplier
Paint colours vary depending on how they are made, and so by sticking to one manufacturer and production process, you can be sure that the products will be based on similar raw materials and therefore share the same characteristics and a similar look.

Use large areas of colour
Don't paint woodwork in a different colour unless you are fortunate enough to have generous, moulded architraves, skirting boards and window frames. The narrow and rather mean mouldings and characterless windows used in many modern houses won't stand up to the scrutiny of a contrasting colour, so paint them the same colour as the wall and use another colour on the door or window reveal instead.

Keep furnishings to a minimum
The vivid scene is really is for those with minimalist tendencies as clutter will turn fantasy into horror. And don't attempt this if your furniture is not up to scratch. Far from drawing attention away from sub-standard stuff, a bold colour scheme will show up all its deficiencies.

Don't forget the floor
Extending the colour scheme to the floor will make the look more cohesive. If your existing floor is beautiful wood, stone or tiles, think about using colourful rugs, but if the floor is not special, then you could paint it or put down a rubber or vinyl floor covering.

Above: The brilliant pink throw gives the antique sofa a modern twist as does the unusual colour scheme in this beautiful old house.

Opposite: Many would consider this wild and exuberant colour scheme to be disrespectful to a house such as this, but in fact it creates a joyous ambience, which celebrates the wonderful architectural detailing.

Purple Prose

A house with superb architectural features and detailing responds well to being decorated in an extraordinarily bold way. Dark saturated colours create an almost gothic atmosphere and painting a room in plum and black requires a certain amount of courage. You may not have such a distinctive home as the one shown opposite, but you can modify this look to suit more modest surroundings by concentrating on furnishings rather than features. Ornate mirrors, picture frames, chairs, bookcases, sideboards and large dressers are all up for a dramatic transformation. This look is about grand gestures so keep things big – a pared-down interior with a few large, good-looking pieces will work, but filling the place with a lot of brightly coloured small and undistinguished pieces won't. This look is perfect if you have antique furniture, which will look great against these colours; polished wood furniture and floors provide welcome respite from so much excitement.

There is no need for fancy furniture if it is not to your taste, though; just use the colours in a simpler way as part of a dark, rich colour scheme. Paint the walls in a dark, restrained colour such as plum, and use the bright purples, brilliant greens and turquoises sparingly but effectively.

Opposite: This highly polished collection of old kitchen utensils and household items adds an authentic glow to this richly coloured interior.

DRAMATIC INTERVENTIONS

In a sitting room:
- Use a dark, subtly patterned wallpaper instead of paint
- Paint the floor deep purple
- Paint a set of French doors in bright green or turquoise
- Put up brilliantly coloured damask curtains
- Use purple velvets and damasks for upholstery and cushions

In a hallway:
- Paint the front door with a deep turquoise glossy paint
- If you have beautiful wooden banisters, leave them alone; if not, paint them a brlliant jade green
- Paint the longest wall in bright purple, jade or grass green

In a bedroom:
- Use purple velvets, silks and damasks for bedcovers and cushions

- Line dark velvet Roman blinds with bright green or turquoise silk
- Cover a beautiful chair in an extravagant and colourful fabric

In a bathroom:
- Cover the walls in turquoise tiles
- Cover the walls in dark tiles and use brightly coloured towels and accessories
- Paint the floor and/or bath panel in bright green or turquoise
- Paint the door and window frames in brilliant turquoise

In a kitchen:
- Paint old units bright green
- Paint window reveals or one wall bright turquoise
- Paint open shelves and dressers brilliant green
- Paint or cover the floor with a bright colour to match the units

Above right: *The use of bright colours for the window, door frame and even some of the beams transforms this kitchen from something old and traditional into something new and unexpected.*

Right: *The curvy shapes and unusual design of this fabulous doorway are emphasised by the choice of colour and decoration, which may be new although it looks convincingly old.*

MAKE IT WORK FOR YOU

Vivid Scenes

This interior appears to break all the rules of taste and restraint but, though it looks like a cheerful hotch-potch, the choice and use of colour is carefully controlled. There are three basic colours – blue, pink and green, with smaller areas of flesh pink, deep pink and splashes of red, shocking pink and turquoise blue. The reason the colour scheme appears quieter than it should is because the light green, pink and blue are of similar strength, not too bright and with quite a lot of white in them, and therefore don't compete for attention. Also, the floor has been painted in the same pink as the wall – a technique that is guaranteed to create a calmer impression. Of the three colours, the pink is slightly more dominant and for this reason has been confined mostly to the lower parts of the room with the fresher, pale green above to lighten things up. Pale blue, which is also used for some of the furniture, is a perfect antidote to pink and prevents it looking too sugary.

The main attraction of this scheme is that it is relaxed and, despite being part of a large high space, looks undeniably cosy. This is a cheap and easy look to emulate as it contains no expensive fittings and the assortment of furniture is mostly old.

Opposite: *Although several strong colours are used in this cheerful, quirky dining area, the pink, green and pale blue are of similar character and strength, which ensures that the overall effect is surprisingly calm.*

COLOUR PALETTE

Raspberry pink	Strawberry ice-cream	Light blue	Light green	Bright blue
An intense colour but its soft tones make it blend rather than shock. It can warm up cooler blues and greens and take the edge off sharp colours such as lime and shocking pink.	*A pale pink tint, a little darker than baby pink and consequently more grown up. On its own it can be a little too sugary so will benefit from being used with fresher colours.*	*A pale blue lightened with white rather than grey. Used on its own it can look cold and wishy-washy, but this fresh, clean colour has an enlivening effect on other colours.*	*This green has similar properties to the light blue but, unlike the blue, can work well on its own with pink. It is a good colour for kitchens and bathrooms.*	*This colour can look harsh on its own, but here, where it is used in small amounts on the table legs and a single chair, it adds weight and contrast and stands out well against the pinks.*

Electric Shocks

Above: *The combination of curves, metallic finishes and brilliant colours bring a touch of fantasy and film-set glamour to this distinctive interior.*

At a time when old is the new 'new', not everyone is in retreat and there are still people willing to embrace the 21st century and all it offers in the way of new materials, sleek design and brilliant colours. We live in an almost super-colourful age, in which technology exposes us to new electronic, 'virtual' colours that exist only by the presence of light. These electrically charged colours on computer and television screens and advertising hoardings may not exist in reality, but new materials and production methods have brought a new range of brilliant colours to the interior-design market. And if these are still not not sharp enough for your taste, then you can always add extra zing in the form of clever lighting.

Synthetic materials are the obvious medium for these types of colours. New developments in paint production allow for more intense hues, and synthetic fabrics and dyes have brought about colours that never existed before. There is also a wide range of materials with metallic, highly polished and high-gloss finishes, and a greater use of glass and acrylics in furniture, fixtures and fittings.

Such materials and colours are naturally suited to a modern, space-age look, but brightly coloured silks and velvets have their own luminosity, which can be used to light up a more traditional style of interior.

Above: *The colours in this elegant sitting room are strong and deep and the velvet used on the sofas and the polished floor reflect the light to enhance the colourful glow.*

ELECTRICAL APPLIANCE

The intensity of these vibrant colours is best represented in high-tech, high-spec, innovative designs and materials. Even if you don't want to spend all day surrounded by luminous colours, sparkling finishes, high-gloss surfaces and the latest technology, you may be more than happy to have them in your kitchen and bathroom.

Kitchens

Glass, metal, shiny surfaces and vibrant, dazzling colours are natural companions, which is why today's functional, sparkling kitchens are an obvious place to go electric. The effect of bright colour will be multiplied by its reflection in glass or polished steel. Look out for tiles with metallic finishes and metal flooring, and think about having slatted metal blinds in a bright colour. Complete the circuit with shiny utensils, aluminium café furniture, glamorous steel-framed bars stools and coloured or transparent acrylic chairs – and lots and lots of light.

Bathrooms

You may prefer something a little more sober in the rest of your home but you can afford to be bold in the bathroom. Bathrooms are a good place to experiment as the solid shapes of white fittings stand out beautifully and provide light relief against bright colours. Also, in a small space, you can often afford to indulge in more expensive materials, especially when it comes to flooring. The sparkly nature of bathrooms is emphasised by shiny taps and shower fittings, which reflect colours brilliantly, as do metallic or white glazed tiles, glass shower cubicles and shelving, chrome and stainless-steel fixtures and fittings. For maximum impact, use electric colours for walls and bath panels as well as for towels and storage containers.

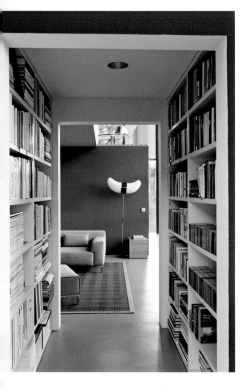

Above: *The ethereal blue seen in this interior can be created using lighting systems rather than paint, with which colours can be changed to suit different moods and requirements.*

Opposite: *The light coming in through the glazed wall illuminates the reflective surfaces of the floor and staircase to add extra brilliance to the colours.*

ELECTRICAL CURRENTS

The white box may not be cutting edge any more but the stark interior still has its appeal, only now it provides an opportunity to use brilliant, clear colours in a disciplined way that emphasises clean lines and uncluttered spaces. Such interiors are suited to intense colours with more than a hint of electric blue, and while they may prove too cold and impersonal for many, for others they create an intentional ambience of cool efficiency.

This approach works very well in an open-plan interior, where different colours can be used to define different areas and functions or draw attention to particular details. Not everyone who loves modern, minimalist interiors is fortunate enough to live in a large, architect-designed house, but dramatic use of colour is a perfect way to turn the mundane into the marvellous. It's all about straight lines, large areas of plain colour and lots of light.

This is a look that works best if it is applied throughout a whole house or apartment – and it is perfect for studio and live–work spaces. Painting a whole space in a light but bright aqua blue may sound extreme, but when one colour is used on every surface, the effect is one of unity and therefore the impression is of calm rather than alarm.

Trick of the light

The way to make bright colours brilliant is to add light, and the way to create colour where none exists is to add coloured light. New developments in lighting allow you to create your own light show at home. Systems are available that change the colours in a room to suit different times of the day, different functions and even different occupants. If you have the desire – and the means – it is possible to have a brilliantly coloured space without using a drop of coloured paint.

ILLUMINATING FACTS

If the high-tech option is out of your range, there are other ways in which you can illuminate your life and home.

- Wall washes direct light up and down a wall to add intensity to any colour.

- The humble wall-light performs a similar role, especially if you use several in a row rather than one or two. Use a row of bulkhead lights to light your way along a hallway, for example.

- Using concealed lighting under cupboards and shelving is a good way to illuminate brightly coloured walls and objects.

- Lights set into the floor are no longer just for public spaces: they look great in a hallway or bathroom or set around the edge of the floor in a living area.

- When you don't need them for studying, aim desk lights at the wall. Simple but effective.

chalky

muted

mellow

limewash

distemper

HISTORICAL

Prussian blue

ASSOCIATIONS

yellow ochre

red ochre

chrome yellow

azure

Despite the fact that we live in a high-tech age, our interest in the past, especially in old houses, has never been greater. There is no doubt that older houses – not only the grand ones but also those of ordinary people – have a restful air about them redolent of a much simpler, and slower, pace of life, which appeals to those of us caught up in frenetic 21st-century lifestyles. The apparent tranquillity of these houses is to some degree due to the mellowing effects of age but also to the muted qualities of the colours used for decoration.

This interest has been picked up by paint manufacturers, resulting in the availability of several 'historic' colour ranges. Some of these manufacturers produce paint using traditional techniques and materials while others supply their versions of 'old' colours in paints made with synthetic additives. The traditionally made paints normally contain more pigment and therefore the colours are more intense, but they are more expensive and more coats are often needed to get an even finish. Modern paints, on the other hand, are cheaper, cover well and are easier to use.

Because there is so much interest in old houses, there is also a lot of information available on the colours used. This is especially useful for devotees of authenticity who wish to re-create the past, but you don't have to be a slave to history – or own a beautiful old house – to appreciate the subtlety and special qualities of the old colours. While it is often homes from the 18th and 19th centuries that attract much of the acclaim, other, more recent styles also have their enthusiasts. From the restraint of Modernism and Art Deco through to the exuberance of the fifties and sixties, each period and style has its own distinctive palettes and ways of using colour.

Right: *This grand interior is treated in a simple but traditional way with the magnificent detailing picked out in gold, which glows beautifully in the romantic lighting.*

Traditional Ingredients

The so-called historic colours, especially those made from traditional ingredients, share similar characteristics, which make them appear softer and more subdued. This is because early paints were made without the synthetic whiteners and brighteners used in modern paints. Instead, they relied on chalk, china clay, barium and lead as lighteners, which gave them the greyish, slightly dirty look that we find so attractive today. Before the 18th century, the number of pigments readily available and affordable was mostly limited to umbers, siennas and yellow ochres. Darker tones were achieved by heating these pigments. It was, therefore, often the lack of ingredients rather than inherent good taste that dictated the colour schemes of the past that we so much admire today.

At one time, only the rich could afford strong colours. This is especially true of blue, which was made from expensive lapis lazuli. However, the development of Prussian blue, along with other newer and less expensive pigments, meant that stronger colours became more common, particularly during the early 19th century, when the discovery of chrome yellow not only provided a bright yellow but also influenced related colours such as blue.

The early 18th century saw the advent of Palladian architecture, which favoured all-white interiors. Although there were plenty of stable red pigments around, red and pink were not fashionable until the mid 18th century. They became so again in early 19th century, when the availability of deeper, brighter reds coincided with the fashion for bright reds as discovered in the ruins of Pompeii and Herculaneum.

It is a mistake to think of historic colours only in terms of the 18th and 19th centuries, however, as there are plenty that refer to movements and styles in the 20th century. The colours of the Art Deco era and the 1950s have their own distinctive colours and colour combinations, and though we tend to associate the Modernists with white, they actually used a lot of bold colours.

Below left: *The muted colouring used on this paintwork is typical of the historical colours that would have been used when the house was built.*

Opposite: *This room could be in a modern home but a sense of history is suggested by the use of colour as well as the old painting and antique sofa.*

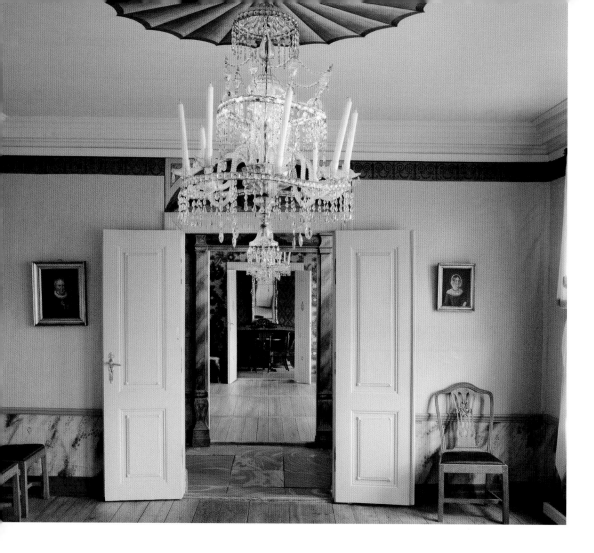

Fine Finishes

The attraction of old paints lies not only in the colours but also in the finish, especially the chalky finish of the old distempers. Several paint manufacturers are producing paints that re-create the dense colours and the flat, matt surfaces used on both walls and paintwork. Colours vary according to the finish: in a high gloss, a colour will look lighter than in a matt finish.

ORIGINAL RECIPES

Paints made according to old methods use natural products with pigments added to give the colour. They normally contain a higher percentage of pigment than modern paints and so have a higher saturation of colour. Despite this, more coats are normally needed in order to build up the colour. One of the biggest advantages of these and other natural paints is that they are porous and therefore allow the wall to 'breathe'. Walls that cannot breathe are a major cause of damp problems in houses so these paints not only look good, they are also good for your home.

Limewash
One of the earliest types of paint, limewash is made from chalk and lime mixed with water. The surface is not very stable and rubs off easily so limewash is normally used only by purists.

Distemper

A similar mix to limewash but containing added binders in the form of glue and casein (milk solids) and sometimes a little linseed oil. This makes the surface more stable, and in some, the amount of chalk is reduced, which results in deeper colours. The big disadvantage of distemper is that you cannot paint over it with any other type of paint.

Shiny finishes

The addition of linseed oil creates a more robust and stable paint with a slightly glossy finish. A hard, durable surface was made possible by the addition of lead, which also had good covering power. Lead is a hazardous material and no longer used in paints, except for very special conservation projects; it has been replaced by safer alternatives such as titanium oxide.

Gloss finishes were often achieved with a separate coat of varnish until a paint with a hard shiny finish was made by adding varnish and omitting 'matting agents'. Some of these oil-based paints require several coats in order to build up the depth of colour and a hard surface, and in order to achieve a good finish, it is also necessary to sand down the surface between coats.

NEW RECIPES

Modern paints contain plasticisers, resins and binders, which, as well as making the paints much easier to use, increase their covering power and allow for much brighter, cleaner colours. They are also less expensive than the so-called traditional paints. For ecological and safety reasons, most paints and primers are now water-based rather than oil or spirit-based.

Emulsion

Emulsion has replaced distemper and is much easier to use. It covers well and has a stable, hard-wearing surface. This water-based paint is available in a huge range of colours and in matt or soft sheen finishes. It is also relatively inexpensive.

Eggshell

This paint gives a semi-matt finish for paintwork. It has a slight sheen that is less shiny than gloss. It is perfect for the more understated look associated with older properties and historical paint techniques and effects.

Gloss

Obtaining a smooth, blemish-free, extra-shiny surface is becoming easier with modern, quick-drying gloss paints, which are formulated for ease of use.

Far left: *The soft sheen finish used on the woodwork here is more appropriate to the style and age of this house than a hard gloss finish would be.*

Below: *The bold paint colours that have been used in this bathroom complement the equally strong character of the fittings and the beautiful tiled floor.*

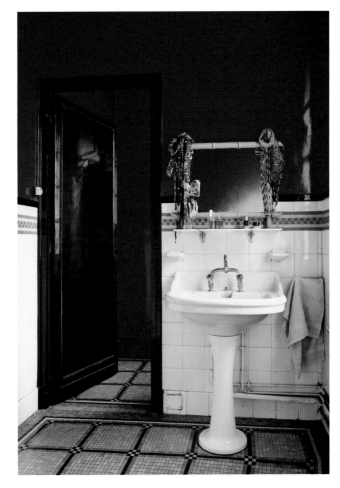

Historically Correct

Below right: *Soft greens and blues were often used in old houses and suit perfectly both the architecture and the type of furnishings of the same era.*

Opposite: *The patina on this wall is probably a combination of the effects of age, lime plaster and the use of a traditionally made paint with a matt, chalky finish.*

When we think of historic colours, it is usually the soft muted hues that come to mind, but although they lack the brilliance made possible with new paints, the darker shades in these ranges are no less dramatic.

Red

Deep tones are produced with pigments such as red ochre and yellow ochre, which can be burnt to produce even darker shades. These earth pigments would have formed the basis of the deep, warm, earthy red found in the ruins of Pompeii and Herculaneum. As the basis of terra cottas and pinks, these tones have long been a staple colour in Mediterranean countries, but they also appear in grand country houses and even Modernist masterpieces. These warm earthy reds work well with deep blue.

Pigments such as vermilion and carmine produce more intense, pure reds, which look equally at home in traditional or modern settings. They also look stunning in a gloss finish.

Cobalt blue

The addition of cobalt creates an intense pure blue familiar from old blue and white china. In a chalky matt finish it recedes and looks darker but in a shiny finish it glows brighter. This is a powerful, dominating colour and works well with white though it can also look sensational with bright yellow.

Pea green

The colour of young or frozen peas rather than the more muted tones of pea soup. A deep colour, which is also clean and clear, this is very versatile in that it can look fresh and modest in simple surroundings or grown-up and sophisticated, especially with gold.

Forest green

A very dark green that is not too sombre as it still has some yellow in it. Forest green can be too overwhelming in large quantities but is a good colour to use if you want contrast without too much drama.

Yellow ochre

Because it is based on the earth pigment, this essentially mellow yellow has warmth rather than brilliance. It has a calming effect on other colours but, thanks to its gentler qualities, stands up well on its own, too, even in large quantities. Old ochres complement old houses but get a new lease of life as hot mustard in contemporary settings.

Chrome yellow

The discovery of chrome yellow led to much brighter shades of yellow that were cooler and lighter than the ochres. Chrome yellow is equally at home as the star of an elegant dining room complete with silk furnishings or in a cheerful modern interior teamed with bright red or blue.

MAKE IT WORK FOR YOU

Historically Correct

Your bedroom may not be quite as impressive as this one but there are plenty of ideas that can be adapted for less distinctive homes. The atmosphere is serene even though five colours have been used, not including the colours in the printed panel. The colours on the walls and panelling are pale and understated and are the types of colours associated with elegant town houses and genteel lifestyles. This is quite an elaborate decoration scheme but the essential elements can be adapted to suit simpler surroundings and tastes.

Panelling was a feature of the grander houses of the 17th and 18th centuries where it was well suited to high ceilings and generous-sized rooms. It is relatively easy to create panels by fixing wooden mouldings to a plain wall, but be careful or it could look rather tacky: use a generous wide moulding and get the work done professionally. Alternatively, create 'panels' in paint only: mark them out carefully and use masking tape to ensure a neat edge. In order to make rooms appear higher, make the panels tall and narrow. In a small room, especially if it has a low ceiling, restrict the number of panels, and if you have a lot of furniture, it might be a good idea to confine the panelling to one clear wall. Dark patterns can be overpowering in a small room so with printed panels, either limit their number or opt for a design with more muted colours.

Opposite: *Despite the elaborate detailing and quite complex decorative scheme, this bedroom still retains an air of tranquil elegance.*

COLOUR PALETTE

Deep blue	Pale apple green	Paler green	Warm pink	Pinky beige
A dark, deep colour that is best used sparingly either as part of a pattern or in a luxurious fabric such as silk or velvet.	*This is a soft green, fresh enough to prevent the pink looking too sweet but pale and subtle enough to be used on paintwork.*	*A lighter, and slightly bluer, shade of the pale apple that is pale enough to look obviously different but not so light that it loses its green-ness.*	*A warm pink with added yellow and a small amount of grey to make it look subtle and sophisticated.*	*A darker shade of pink with added beige. It could look dull on its own but here it adds definition to the pale green and flesh pink.*

ADDED INGREDIENTS

Printed panel
A decorative panel provides a stark contrast to the low-key colours as well as introducing some pattern. These panels may well be fabric but printed wallpaper is an easier option.

Woodwork
You can paint attractive architraves, windows, skirting boards and panelled doors using three colours, as in the room illustrated here. If the room is small, stick to one or two colours only.

Mouldings and cornices
If you are fortunate enough to have decorative mouldings or cornices, paint them in a different colour from the wall.

Furniture
If your room lacks distinguished features, introduce them in the form of furniture. Pick out the detailing on a wardrobe with panelled doors, and add an ornate dressing table or bedhead, or a chest of drawers with the drawer fronts painted a different colour.

Old Character

Old houses often look more comfortable with their original peeling paintwork and patchy walls than they do when they are forced into a clean and tidy coat of paint. 'Distressed' is no longer a polite euphemism for falling on hard times; instead, it has become a declaration of love and respect for the past life and historical credentials of a house. Those who have this respect would no more think of covering the walls of an old house than they would of painting over an original work of art because it didn't match the new colour scheme.

If you are leaving the walls in all their faded glory, it is particularly important that you pay careful attention to the floor finish. As in any interior, a poor-quality or horrible floor can completely spoil the effect. Old or new solid wood floors work best with this look; laminates are not so good. Although bare floors will naturally complement this style, carpet can work too, especially the natural fibres such as sea grass and sisal. Oriental rugs and kelims are other obvious choices, as are large mats made from natural fibres and bound with cotton webbing. Modern rugs in plain or bold designs won't look out of place either.

Some people who have a natural affinity with this look can happily furnish a room with a battered and torn collection of furniture and artefacts and make it look wonderful, but for others, the look is more difficult to achieve, and there is a fine line between distressed and disastrous! It mustn't look simply as though you haven't bothered to decorate and neither is the style an excuse for neglect or scruffiness. As with most good interior schemes, discipline, tidiness and cleanliness will help make it work.

The nature of old paintwork and walls means that though they are full of character, the colours are broken and undefined, so using a carefully thought-out colour scheme will complement the beauty of the old surfaces and act as a focus against the muted background.

OLD FLATTERERS

White
One of the easiest ways to flatter these old interiors is with white; not a hard, blue-white but the soft white of unbleached cotton and linen. White upholstered chairs and sofas, especially if they are pretty shapes, look fabulous against an old wall. Off-white rugs and mats, blinds, simple curtains and white table linen or bedlinen complete the picture. Choose thick cottons and linens or, if you want a grander look, self-striped fabrics and damasks.

Pink
Old plaster is normally either pink or grey so pink is a good choice for keeping the atmosphere warm and calm. Go for salmon pink with another deeper pink and add touches of burnt orange, muted red and pale yellowy lime. For contrast, you could try dark grey. These earthy colours work beautifully in velvet and thick cottons as well as the cottons and wools of mats and kelims, where they are often used in combination.

Past and present
Sleek contemporary furniture looks fabulous in an old setting, but take care with the colour. It may be tempting to use bright colours, but the pristine perfection of modern furniture is enough of a contrast so opt for strong, muted, historic colours such deep red, azure blue, emerald green and golden yellow.

Opposite: It takes courage to leave surfaces in their unfinished state, but here the distressed walls celebrate both the age of the building and the unusual curved ceiling.

CHARACTER DEVELOPMENT

If you have a suitably distressed wall
worth keeping, clean up the surfaces to
get rid of loose paint, dust and any
obvious blobs of dirt, then seal the
surface with wax or vanish. If there any
large holes, simply fill them in – they
will add to the character.

If, however, you have pristine walls
but long for something more interesting,
there are things you can do. Painting
your own distressed surface is not easy,
so unless you are skilled in the art
department, either employ a professional
or stick to something simpler.

Colour washes

Putting colour 'washes' on a wall is a
way of building an interesting surface
that has a slightly uneven distribution
of colour. The technique involves using
several coats of very thin, watered-down
paint, so, depending on what colours
you choose, paint the wall first in an

ordinary emulsion. A white background
is too stark, so choose a softer colour:
the muted greys and greens are good
or you could use a pink that is close to
the colour of bare plaster.

These easy recipes use artists'
paints as the base of the colour wash.
The water-based wash is easier to use
than the glaze, but both methods
produce results that are unpredictable,
so be prepared to carry out lots of
tests in an inconspicuous area before
starting on the whole wall or room.

Wash

Add a good squeeze of artists' gouache
or acrylic paint to a small amount of
emulsion paint, add water and mix
thoroughly in order to avoid blotchiness.
It is best if each coat is of the same
strength, so measure out the amounts
you use so that you can make further
batches if necessary. Apply the wash
using a large brush – it doesn't have to
be applied evenly but it shouldn't be
too patchy either so paint in large
strokes across the wall. Each coat will
show through to the next, creating an
uneven, 'distressed' look. Put on as
many coats of paint as necessary to
achieve the desired effect. Water-based
washes should be sealed with varnish.

Glaze

This is a more ambitious project that will
give a similar effect to a wash but with
a glazed surface. As it involves the use
of oil, it is more difficult to apply than
a water-based wash and, consequently,
the results may be more unpredictable.

Make up the glaze using one part
commercial oil glaze to three parts of
white spirit, plus one tablespoon of
white undercoat or eggshell per every
half a litre. Add the tint in the form of
artists' oil paint; the amount you use
will depend on the depth of colour you
require. As with the wash, remember to
measure out the colour in order to get
the right strength in further batches.

Left : *The use of
orange paint on
the wall ties in
the old, worn
paintwork on the
shutters to the
cheerful floral
print on the
chairs.*

Opposite: *Even
more character
has been added to
this room with
trompe-l'oeil paint
effects. The
beautiful, subtle
colour scheme
appears to have
been inspired by
the colours in
the kilim.*

Old Colour, New Look

Historic colours don't have to be used in traditional ways; they are, after all, beautiful colours in their own right and therefore well worth using in modern settings too. The benefit of perusing historic paint charts is that they will provide you with an edited selection of colours that share similar qualities and which therefore, on the whole, naturally work well with one another. This is particularly true of the traditionally made paints, whose similar tones derive from the fact that they are all made from the same base of natural ingredients and pigments.

In modern buildings, architects and interior designers have started using much more colour than they did in the past. This is partly because many materials are now available in better and more sophisticated colours than ever before, but also because there is more of an appetite for colour among consumers. Modern design is often associated with bright intense colours but many designers also appreciate the depth of colour, muted tones and matt finishes that are associated with the historic paints. The dark colours, in particular, have great strength but also great subtlety, unlike modern, brilliant colours, which tend to make their presence felt in a loud way.

These old colours and paints are also much kinder to modern homes, which often have little character and no distinguishing features. In addition, new paints, which contain less pigment and therefore have a less dense colour, are made using synthetics, which produce an even finish that can be unforgiving and more likely to highlight imperfections. The soft chalky colours and textures of old-fashioned paints smooth over the rough edges and create a gentler ambience.

Opposite: *Whatever the style and age of a house, using old-style paints and colours can create an atmosphere that is subdued without being in any way gloomy.*

Right: *Pink is not an easy colour to use on walls, but here it is freshened up with pale green, turquoise and white to create a look that is grown-up and sophisticated.*

rubies

emeralds

amber

tapestries

medieval

RICH TAPESTRY

old masters

Persian rugs

kelims

candlelight

Surrounding yourself with the comfort of textiles, textures and pattern is the perfect antidote to clean, minimal living. It's a look that many would consider old-fashioned, but in fact it's beyond fashion, a style that has existed in slightly different forms for hundreds of years. In grand stately homes, the wall-hangings and drapery are an affirmation of the wealth of the owner as much as of good taste, as well as evidence of patronage and travel.

However, the rich tapestry of life is also to be found in more modest surroundings such as cosy parlours, where pattern creates a friendly habitat for warm relations and tea and sympathy. In traveller's caravans, lack of space is no deterrent to turning the interior into a veritable patchwork quilt of treasured possessions. The patterns of the Orient and of Africa never go out of fashion and their influence can be seen in both old and contemporary textiles. Floral patterns, too, are always popular in some form, whether spriggy prints or big splodgy flower shapes and geometric plant life.

How you use your pattern permit is up to you. If you choose to leave no surface uncovered, swathing furniture in rugs and throws and floors with kelims and Persian rugs, that's fine. If you favour a more restrained use of pattern, then add richness with colour. However, while a joyful jumble of coloured patterns can work for some people, not everyone can do it. If you're in doubt, keep a colour theme running through the different designs and use pattern in specific places, leaving areas of plain colour to give them a chance to breathe and to stand out. Use what you have and what you like, and don't be afraid to put together your own personal style. It could even reawaken an interest in sewing and knitting – a huge wall-hanging may be out of your league, but you could start with some needlepoint cushion covers.

Right: *The tapestry wall-hanging completes the picture and adds to the aura of richness and texture in this opulent room.*

Passion for Pattern

It's good to be able to use patterns again without incurring the wrath of the style police and the anti-clutter detectives, and a relief to eschew the plain and simple and the pared down in favour of something a little more decorative and even busy. Whether you go for classic or retro, floral or geometric, ethnic or Oriental, there is no shortage of fabrics, wallpapers, carpets, ceramics and accessories to tempt you back to pattern. You could even reinstate the chintz!

Putting pattern centre stage needs a bit of careful direction, however. The difficulty lies not so much in making it look good than in avoiding it appearing too considered – the days of mix-and-match co-ordinates are over, but with so many different types of design and colours to choose from, it can be difficult to create organised chaos rather than a disorganised mess.

Print works
A fresh way of using prints is to choose those with dark or coloured backgrounds and set them in a bright, bold setting that is more gypsy caravan than country cottage, and more French Provençal than toiles de Jouy. If you deliberately choose patterns that contain little or no white, the colours will appear more solid and therefore more dramatic.

Flower power
Rather like a wild, unkempt garden, a mixture of different floral fabrics somehow works. It does help if they have some colours in common, but if not, you can link them by picking out some of their main colours and using them as plain fabrics or paint colours. Try to have a mix of large and small patterns and opt for dark backgrounds.

Retro heaven
The patterns from a specific era will all share a similar look, not only because of the designs and colours but also because of the types of dyes and fabrics used. The popular patterns of the fifties are gloriously colourful and love to be part of a crowd. Although they enjoy the company of furniture and artefacts from the same era, they are equally happy with other styles.

Pattern pending
Not everyone wants or likes an excess of pattern or decoration, and those who favour the more pared-down, modern approach may prefer their patterns to be kept under control. However, it is possible to invoke rich tapestry with colour, texture and a few well-chosen extras. Try richly coloured walls, sleek furniture in plain-coloured textured fabrics and a single beautiful rug hung on the wall, for example.

MAKE IT WORK FOR YOU

Passion for Pattern

If you are looking for an opportunity to indulge your passion for prints then the ideal place to start is a bedroom. This cosy niche is prevented from being twee by the use of deep, warm red paint and a dark print. The fact that the colours make the place feel small is of no consequence – its smallness is its biggest feature.

The printed dado is an unusual touch that adds to the quirkiness. The choice of a dark-coloured print balances the colour of the wall above and prevents things looking top heavy. For a really cosy effect, the dado has become an extended padded headboard made from fabric, but a printed wallpaper could give a similar effect.

There is an orderliness in this neat sleeping area that gives the impression that there is a place for everything and everything is in its place. The bed is covered with an eclectic collection of fabrics and quilts in which the colour theme is predominantly dark or at least quiet. The cushions are neatly arranged, and even the assemblage of pictures, pretty shelves and objects fixed to the wall look organised. The plain, functional shelves are painted the same colour as the walls and so stay in the background. The jolly, patterned containers also share a similar style and colouring.

Opposite: *The use of predominantly dark colours, especially on the walls, ensures that the overall impression is dramatic rather than pretty.*

COLOUR PALETTE

Deep red	**Bright red**	**Deep turquoise**	**Pink**
An intense, warm yet muted colour that is relaxing rather than stimulating. Because it is an earthy colour, this deep red goes with almost any other colour and won't dominate.	*This bright red can be found in all types of design and patterns. It is therefore a useful colour to use in bringing together a diverse collection of prints and patterns.*	*A rich, deep colour that is nevertheless bright and cheerful. With the red, this colour on its own would be too strong, but as part of a print that contains red it retains its power without overwhelming.*	*This clean, deep pink appears in several of the floral patterns here, where it provides a lighter, fresher alternative to bright or deep red.*

ADDED INGREDIENTS

Bedcovers
Pretty floral bedlinen blends in with the
surroundings better than pure white.
Use a plain bedcover underneath then
add layers of fabric remnants, table
cloths, old curtains or patchwork quilts.
For other dark, bold patterns, look at
African prints, as well as Chinese and
Japanese fabrics, which often have a lot
of red and black in them.

Storage
Make pretty containers earn their place
and use them as useful storage. If you
need more space, you could have a
large trunk, either painted or covered
with patterned fabric. If wardrobes and
chests of drawers are spoiling the
effect, paint them to match the walls. If
they look too plain, stick printed paper
on the drawer and door fronts.

Extras
These delightful shelves and pictures
are the sort of things you find in junk
shops and antique markets. If you have
a more disparate collection of objects,
you could paint some of them to bring
them together, but don't do everything
or it will look too self-conscious.

Dramatic dark interiors resemble these blackened oil paintings with their copious use of dark browns and almost blacks, and glimpses of brilliant colours in the form of fabric or perhaps paint. Dark interiors don't have to be gloomy: they can have an air of mystery or grandeur but still be surprisingly restful.

DARK INSPIRATIONS

Medieval hall

Imagine rooms hung with red tapestries and the comfort of roaring fires and pewter goblets filled with warm red wine. You can emulate the austerity of the baronial hall with plain, but beautiful furniture, wood and flagstone floors, patterned carpets and wall-hangings. Along with the colours of stone and dark polished wood, use the reds, greens and blues of heraldry plus the earthy, muted tones of tapestries.

French château and English country house

If you like your dark a little more refined, the elegance of country houses and châteaux may be more to your taste. Lighten the dark with ornate furniture and chandeliers. Think of emerald-green and deep azure-blue silks and brocades set against a black background with flattering candlelight.

The soukh

It is difficult to think of anywhere else that you will find such a plethora of elaborate patterns and rich colours, from the deep colourings of Oriental carpets to the browns, ochres, reds and soft indigo of kelims. Yet despite their variety, they all share the subtle earthy quality characteristic of natural pigments. However, there are flashes of bright colours here too, and they provide the sort of contrast that makes the image of a pair of bright pink silk slippers on a Persian carpet such a pleasing one.

Old Masters

Above: *The beautiful silk damask glows wonderfully in this glorious, mainly golden, sumptuous interior.*

Opposite: *A white chair stands out beautifully against the dark, dramatic wallpaper, which, together with dark paintwork, brings an opulent, rich feel to this room.*

The masters of interior design have for centuries taken their inspiration from paintings. Some aim to capture the cool serenity of Vermeer's interiors, others are seduced by drapery or elaborate furnishings, and a few take their lead from still life. But all are influenced by the colours. Centuries ago, the pigments available to painters for mixing colours were limited to naturally occurring ones, most of which derive from the earth and so share an earthy quality. In addition, the varnishes used to protect the finished works contained oils that blacken over time, giving the paintings a sombre, glistening appearance with only the brightest colours shining through.

Opposite: *The brown walls, richly patterned floor and chandelier add to the mysterious, almost magical ambience in this uncompromisingly dark, narrow passageway.*

DARK BROWN STUDY

Brown is a colour often associated with gloomy old houses and dirt. It is also the disappointing colour you got as a child when you mixed all those lovely bright colours together in your paintbox. Brown is often thought of as a dreary colour, but like those small brown birds whose plumage appears boring at a distance, a closer look reveals an unimagined variety of subtle colourings that is anything but dull. Indeed, brown can be chic: cool grey-browns are a popular choice for modern furniture, where dark, heavily grained wood is fashionable, and smooth brown upholstery looks smart and sophisticated. Dark brown is the colour of wood darkened with age, as well as of bitter and milk chocolate, rich loamy soil and dry bracken.

Brown is also often considered to be gloomy, but as the ultimate earth colour, it is close to nature and therefore a peaceful and relaxing colour. However, too much brown can be depressing as well as dark. Unless you have huge, lofty rooms, it is best to confine brown to one wall or enjoy it as the rich, mellow tones of polished wood on floors, furniture and even ceilings and walls.

Chocolate box

If you want to know what goes with delicious chocolate brown, imagine a box of chocolates decorated with bright pink, yellow, green and violet sugar flowers. Then again, it looks good with white chocolate too!

Brown sugar

From demerara to dark muscovado, from the golden shine of toffee and butterscotch to the softer matt of fudge, these sweeter browns are delicious, but you may need to add white elsewhere in the scheme to cleanse the palate.

A touch of brown

From buff to beige and bone to stone, these so-called 'neutral' colours all contain a hint of brown, which gives them their warmth. The tiniest amount of added brown can turn white into cream and take the edge off red. Greige is a chic version of beige and contains brown and grey. It is a wonderfully understated colour, as is taupe, which has an added touch of green. Undyed natural fibres also have a brownish tinge, which gives natural fabrics their muted appearance.

BROWNIE POINTS

Brown may be a strong colour, but it is also versatile – you can change its mood depending on what colours you put with it.

Hot
Yellow browns are a bit much – it is better to warm up a cooler brown with mustard, burnt orange and chilli red.

Mellow
Chill out and watch those browns mellow with deep blushing pinks and golden yellows.

Cool
Brown can look too warm and woolly. Sharpen it up with turquoise and lime green or smarten it up with pale aqua and pale blue.

Embarrassment of Riches

The owners of stately homes and country houses were certainly not embarrassed by their riches, and neither should you be. This is your opportunity to defy the light and airy brigade and surround yourself with the comfort of drapery and napery. Enjoy flowery wallpaper, layers of curtains, bits of lace, velvets, chenille, old carpets and displays of pretty china. Go ahead and cover tables with cloths, drape old chairs with kelims, pile on the bedcovers, hang rugs on the wall – and if you were looking for an excuse to have swags and drapes, this could be it. The look may be reminiscent of a century ago, but it doesn't have to be old stuff – modern, simple shapes and clean lines are a good foil to prevent things getting out of hand. If you want ornament and pattern, there is plenty in the shops that is decorative. This is one time when an overly considered colour scheme could spoil the effect. Go with your instincts, but avoid very bright colours – stick to the more muted shades, and enjoy!

RICH INGREDIENTS

Patterned wallpaper
The perfect opportunity to smother the walls in pattern, especially as there are now so many gorgeous designs on the market. Avoid white backgrounds, a lot of white, very wild colours or very large designs. The Arts and Crafts' style has the right sort of richness of colour and pattern, but there are also other designs inspired by bygone eras to choose from.

Oriental carpets
It's well known that these classic carpets will fit in with almost any style or colour scheme. Threadbare is fine and layers are even better.

Treasured possessions
Minimalism has made us nervous of putting our possessions on display for fear of revealing our real character, but now is the time to get out the patterned china and finally put all those pictures on the wall. A wall of books will add colour and texture.

Above: This highly individual interior conforms to no specific style, but it does demonstrate the owners' passion for colour, pattern and textiles.

Opposite: The splendid wall-hanging, together with the decorative table, ornamented chair and harp, creates a wonderfully rich and rather theatrical setting.

NOUVEAU RICHES

If you don't have trunks of old fabrics and draperies that have been waiting for a fashion moment to see the light of day again, you can always buy new versions, often very cheaply, at high-street and chain stores, markets and the large furniture warehouses.

- **Curtaining** – as well as fabrics you can choose from a huge selection of ready-made and second-hand curtains plus window panels in lace and muslin.

- **Throws** – all kinds, from tartan and velvet to ethnic embroideries and patchwork.

- **Quilts** – not only as bedcovers, but also for walls, windows, sofas and chairs.

- **Rugs** – plenty of kelims and dhurries, rag rugs, Oriental-style rugs and carpets, which, like quilts, also look good on chairs, sofas, beds and walls.

Jewel Personality

Deep, rich colours with an inner glow bring to mind precious stones such as emeralds, rubies, sapphires, amethysts and topaz, all with a common purpose – to dazzle and flatter. When choosing the contents of your own jewel box, make sure your jewels have the beauty and depth of the real thing rather than the more brash sparkle of costume jewellery. Genuine stones can be mixed together without looking vulgar as their quality always shines through.

JEWEL BOX

Amethyst, ruby and garnet

Royal purples and regal reds look grand and expensive, especially in velvets, silks and damasks, and are perfect for an elegant and grown-up sitting room, dining room or bedroom. The deeper colours have a natural air of sobriety,

which makes them suitable for places where relaxation is the main activity. Colours at the purple end of the spectrum need to look expensive, so make sure they are not too harsh and cheap looking. To avoid things becoming too overpowering, keep furnishings simple and introduce lighter colours such as pale amethyst, citrine and aquamarine. To spark things up a bit, introduce some diamond brightness with glass and clear acrylic furniture, crystal chandeliers and white linens.

Topaz and amber

These soft, mellow colours are gentler and lend themselves to elegant settings with touches of gold. They will glow in silks and damask wallpapers but look ethnic and earthy in coarse linens and chunky wool. If the look gets a bit heavy and syrupy, freshen it up with silver and aquamarine. If you want something hotter, add garnets and dark amethyst.

Sapphire, aquamarine and turquoise

Blue colours have a reputation for being cool, but cool also implies chic and elegant. These colours suit an 18th-century town-house style and look wonderful with silver and diamond crystal, but they can also be lively, and bring a splash of brilliance to modern interiors, where they sparkle with shiny metal. In their paler forms, they have a low-key serenity and freshness.

Jade and emerald

The nature of these greens gives them depth and variation, which is why they look good in velvet and silk. Because they are quite dark and powerful, they are better in a supporting role than as the main attraction. Use with amethysts, rubies, garnets and gold, and brighten them up with citrines and diamonds.

Below left: *These magnificent, emerald silk embroidered drapes glow like jewels in their dark, richly furnished environment.*

Opposite: *The unusual light source, which resembles an illuminated pearl necklace, throws out just enough light to turn the beads on the floaty fabric into twinkling jewels.*

MAKE IT WORK FOR YOU

Jewel Personality

Though your home may not be as grand as this one, it is possible to create a jewel-box ambience in even the most prosaic room by using a relatively small palette and carefully chosen accessories. There is a lot of colour in this room yet the overall impression is of serenity. A strong green is the background to a richly patterned wallpaper and so shares some of its glory with the floral pattern, and its light-reflecting sheen softens the colour. Green is tempered by touches of ruby red, a colour scheme also echoed in the carpet, and gold. The paintwork is a pale colour rather than white (which would look too stark) and the wooden floor has a mellowing effect. The room is not cluttered and the floor cushions and table keep a low profile so as not to confuse the eye or detract from the stunning wallpaper. The cushions are a softer green and act as a foil to the brilliance of the walls and help to create a sense of calm. For best effect, keep to a relatively small palette of colours, paint the woodwork in a paler version of the colour rather than white, choose colours that blend with the main colour rather than contrast, and avoid overcrowding the room.

Opposite: *The light from the fire and candles adds the final sparkling jewel touch to this room, but even without it, the colours of the furnishings and wallpaper will retain a warm glow.*

COLOUR PALETTE

Emerald	Moss green	Pale green	Ruby	Gold
Strong greens can dominate a room and also make it look dark, so when choosing paint, think about using a soft sheen or eggshell, or a slightly paler version if you want a matt finish.	*The softer, greyer tones of mossy greens will help tone down any brash tendencies of sparkling emerald, and the paler shades are perfect for paintwork.*	*Pale greens that contain a hint of grey look subtle and sophisticated, especially when used in an eggshell finish. Using them as an alternative to white on the woodwork will help to bring a sense of calm to a room.*	*Red and green can be difficult together but here their jewel-like quality unites and harmonises. Red will warm up green but use it sparingly so that it complements rather than competes for attention.*	*Jewels are set in gold for the good reason that it highlights them beautifully, which is why gilt-framed mirrors and pictures work so well. Gold in fabric form is effective too, but think topaz and amber rather than yellow.*

Coventry Central Library

Tel: 024 7683 2314
Fax: 024 7683 2440
Computer Booking: 024 7683 2583

Borrowed Items 27/11/2013 12:03
XXXXXXXXXX9609

Item Title	Due Date
enemy	09/12/2013
Rage of angels	09/12/2013
* Colour	08/01/2014

Amount Outstanding: £5.06

* indicates items borrowed today

Thankyou for using this unit - Cenself03
www.coventry.gov.uk/libraries
email:central.library@coventry.gov.uk
Monday, Tuesday, Wednesday, Thursday
Friday 9.00am - 8.00pm
Saturday 9.00am - 4.30pm
Sunday 12.00noon - 4.00pm

ADDED INGREDIENTS

Wallpaper
A heavily patterned wallpaper all over a small room can look sensational as long as you allow it to take centre stage and keep everything else under control. An alternative is to paper just one wall and paint the rest in a softer shade of the dominant colour in the wallpaper.

Mirrors
As well as adding to the overall richness of a room, a gilt-framed mirror will make the space feel larger and will double the power of the lighting.

Oriental carpets
Despite their elaborate patterns and rich colourings, Oriental carpets seem to go with anything. Old ones are the best as the dyes used are natural and have a mellower tone.

Flattering light
Throughout history, jewels have always responded well to candlelight and firelight, which also impart a flattering and romantic glow to a jewel-inspired interior. A chandelier adds grandeur as well as a gentler form of light.

Oriental Opulence

You don't have to travel extensively to bring Oriental opulence to your home; there are plenty of treasure chests waiting to be plundered in high-street shops and antique emporia throughout the land. Choose from the sumptuous embroideries of India, the brilliant colours of Thailand and the elaborate patterned silks of China. Many of the colours are gloriously gaudy and guaranteed to cheer up any room.

This is an opportunity to adopt a different way of working with colour, by using artefacts rather than colour charts as your source and guide. Whether you adopt a 'go-for-it' attitude or a more considered approach will depend on your personal taste and pattern tolerance threshold, but whether you opt for a riot or an orderly gathering, it is sure to be an enriching experience.

Orient excess

Decorative artefacts of diverse styles and from various parts of the world often share an exuberance and artlessness that enables them to overcome their differences and work together in a sort of chaotic harmony. You might get away with a jolly jumble of prints, embroideries, decorative furniture and artefacts, but to create a medley rather than a mess, it is wise to place things in groups rather than at random, and to mix in some plain colours too. Too many garish colours could be uneasy on the eye, so make sure you include some of the subtler tones. Don't allow special or more beautiful items to get lost in the crowd; give them space to breathe and the attention they deserve.

Transcendental meditation

Opulence doesn't have to involve excess. If you prefer a more Zen approach to the Orient, choose just a few items or colours and make them the focus of attention in a simpler, more pared-down scheme.

This style is particularly suited to traditional Chinese black and red lacquered furniture and accessories, which should be used in a minimal way and look best when arranged in ordered fashion according to tradition, and perhaps the rules of feng shui. An impression of opulence can be created with a single swathe of brilliant red silk, or suggested by a pile of richly coloured, embroidered cushions. A more subtle, though no less opulent ambience is possible with more subdued colourings, as in a room filled with old and faded furniture, furnishings, carpets and wall-hangings.

Opposite: *Whatever size or style of room, this brilliant red embroidered silk and charming lacquered table is sure to create an ambience of exotic opulence.*

Below: *The Orient provides a rich source of treasures. Sometimes just one is enough to provide the inspiration for a whole interior.*

chalks

pastel

unbleached

quiet

Morandi

PALE AND
alabaster
INTERESTING

driftwood

natural

restful

With the pace of life showing no obvious signs of slowing down, our homes have often become a sanctuary, a place to relax, unwind and restore our equilibrium. The restorative qualities of an interior will be enhanced if the ambience is one of calm simplicity with as few distractions as possible, and it goes without saying that an interior that is pale and interesting will be more restful than one that is a riot of colour.

One of the best things about many of the new paint, fabric and wallpaper ranges is the variety and subtlety of the lighter colours, which can be used successfully in a colour scheme suitable for any style or mood, whether in a country cottage, an elegant house or a strikingly modern interior. Subtle, pale colours soften spaces and are kind to your home, and unlike pure white, which can highlight imperfections, slightly darker tones can play them down and make them less conspicuous. They are also more respectful of distinctive architecture and features and will take the hard edges off new properties.

Soft, muted colours help to create a wonderfully harmonious atmosphere, which, though it may not be as light as with white, is nevertheless very calm and restful. However, pale isn't necessarily all about serenity: it can also be smart and crisp. Some of the paler, grungier colours are extremely fashionable and can look cool and sophisticated when used in conjunction with modern furnishings in a pared-down interior.

The options for making pale interesting include a monochrome approach, using one colour only plus shades and tones of it, or a more colourful style, where several colours of similar quality and strength are used to create a slightly livelier atmosphere that is neverthless refreshingly calming.

Opposite: *Painting a witty trompe-l'oeil mural is a good way to make an otherwise minimal interior appear more human and less severe.*

Spatial Harmony

It is a well known decorating fact that painting a whole house or collection of rooms in one colour will unify the space as well as making it feel more spacious. White, or white with a hint of something, has traditionally been the unifying colour of choice, but while white does the job quite efficiently, it can sometimes look too stark, especially in older properties. These days, fortunately, there is a much wider and more interesting selection of pale colours from which you can choose to create harmonious interiors.

Opting for a monochrome scheme means using just one colour, but this is not as restrictive as it sounds as the palette also contains all the tints, tones and shades of that colour, thus providing plenty of scope for a colour scheme that is harmonious without being monotonous. One of the benefits of new paint colours is that there are now many more gradations within each colour, making it easier to choose and use a monochrome palette.

Texture and finish also provide tonal variety. Paintwork in gloss or eggshell will look paler than a matt wall in the same colour, and textiles in similar colours but different textures will also add light and shade.

Incorporating floors and furnishings into a monochrome theme will ensure a thoroughly restrained ambience, but if you want a little more variety, you can add other colours that are similar in tone and quality to the main colour. Being disciplined in your colour scheme doesn't mean that you need to be a minimalist capable of maintaining a completely clutter-free zone – the monochrome look can cope with a comfortable amount of stuff, though it will help if objects on display also comply with the colour theme.

LIGHT TOUCH

To complete the pale and interesting
picture, it is important that your
furnishings blend in and don't spoil the
atmosphere. White is an obvious
choice, with unbleached cottons and
linens for upholstery, plain white cotton
or wool rugs, white curtains and blinds
and white-painted furniture. If white
looks too stark, you could use the very
palest versions of the chosen colour.
Alternatively, if you want textural relief,
stripped or unpainted wood works well.

Opposite, top:
*While white can
look stark and cold,
adding just a hint
of blue, as here, will
give an interior a
gentler feel and a
more interesting
ambience.*

Opposite, bottom:
*With so many doors
and so much glass,
this space could
seem cold and
inhospitable, but
the use of a pale
tint and a matt
finish brings unity
and an air of
serenity to the space.*

Above: *The use of
one basic colour
throughout keeps
things simple here.
Even the objects on
the unusual, ornate
dresser conform to
a strict colour code.*

The New Pastels

There was a time when pastel shades were mostly limited to pale blue, baby pink, primrose yellow, and lilac – the colours of sugared almonds, and a little too sweet for modern tastes. Whereas the old pastels were often confined to nurseries and children's rooms, new pastels are suitable for adult use throughout the whole house. These new colours are more intense, and whereas the old versions were whitened variants of darker colours, the new ones are more complex and therefore much more subtle. They are more like artists' oil pastels, which contain quite a lot of pigment and produce a dense matt finish. Among these new pastels are pale ochres, dusty pinks, chalky blues, khaki greens and dove greys.

One advantage of the new pastels is that, providing you choose those with a similar quality and colour saturation, you can use several together without upsetting the balance, allowing you to create different atmospheres and colour schemes that suit different settings as well as the varying personal tastes of others who share your home. Although they are essentially pale, the colours nevertheless have character, so that even those who want to upset the balance with a more lively colour scheme may be persuaded to accept something more subtle. Little girls may want sugar pink in their bedrooms but might settle for dusty or 'ointment' pink, and most boys would appreciate grungy, 'dirty' green.

Opposite: The muted, greyish tones shown here typify the new pastel shades, which look soft yet sophisticated. Here, they complement beautifully the decorative detailing on the chest and mirror.

TONED DOWN

There are lots of ways to use several muted tones together to create something that is colourful yet quiet.

- Rather than using white or a paler version of the main colour, paint windows, doors, skirting boards and floors a different colour from the walls.

- If your woodwork is not up to much, paint it the same colour as the walls and add interest in the form of a border of a different colour around a door or a window. Ensure that it is quite wide so that it makes a bold statement.

- Large expanses of wall, such as in a hall or on a staircase, often have a dado complete with dado rail, which is the perfect excuse to use two different colours. Put the 'heavier' colour below and the lighter one above. If you don't have a dado, you can create one with paint.

- Stencils have had a bad press, but if you use colours that are very similar they turn from twee into something sophisticated. Don't dot them around, though, and instead of applying them as borders, use large designs such as huge bunches of flowers, or cover the wall in an all-over damask or geometric pattern.

- Painted furniture looks great in the new pastel colours, which are not only perfect for old furniture but also soften the edges and add character to new pieces.

Raw Materials

The high-tech, high-spec, fast-moving world we now live in has left many people longing for a less complicated way of life. Unfortunately, for most of us, the simple life is just not a realistic option; nevertheless, our homes can offer peace and respite in the form of clutter-free, peaceful interiors created using natural materials.

An affinity with nature is often associated with wellbeing, and the use of natural materials in the home can indeed create a particularly harmonious atmosphere. Such materials will inevitably share certain qualities, and many have a gentle, subtle coloration that is enhanced by textures and the non-uniformity that is found, for example, in wood grain and the natural imperfections of stone. While some stones, such as granite and slate, have dark colourings, most have a mellow appearance.

By using natural materials in their raw state we can appreciate their qualities even more and their presence helps to create a back-to-nature feel, which many find relaxing and restorative. This simplicity is redolent of Zen-inspired interiors, where there are no extraneous objects to distract the mind. Such spaces suggest austerity, yet appear, and feel, restful rather than bleak.

Left: *Natural materials have an inherent beauty, as can be seen in the textures, colours and raw qualities of the stone and wood used in this very simple washroom.*

Opposite: *The rough, characterful brickwork gives a rustic, utilitarian look to this unusual kitchen, which is enhanced by the industrial-sized sink and basic fittings.*

RAW INGREDIENTS

Natural fibres

The choice of materials is wide: think about cottons and linens for upholstery and curtains, simple window panels and blinds, while for floors, you could use rush matting, sea-grass, sisal, jute, coir or even paper.

Wool

Creamy, unbleached wool fabrics are great for upholstery, curtaining and throws, and wool is an obvious option for floors, too, in the form of chunky woven mats and tufted woollen rugs and carpets.

Linoleum and rubber

Both linoleum and rubber are made from natural ingredients, and both have a warmth and offer endless possibilities for colour and design.

Willow, rattan and bamboo

These tough grasses provide a lighter alternative to wood for chairs, tables, footstools, ottomans and even shelving, not to mention accessories such baskets, mats and bamboo blinds.

Stone

There are numerous types to choose from, including limestone, slate, shiny marble and granite. Stone is good not only for floors but also for sinks, baths and basins, splashbacks and surrounds. The main ingredient of ceramic tiles is clay so they are another natural alternative for floors and walls.

Wood

Wood is one of the most ubiquitous and versatile natural materials and has intrinsically beautiful properties. Make the most of its mellow presence in floors, furniture and slatted wooden blinds as well as in structural features such as beams, staircases, windows, doors, architraves and skirting boards.

Faded Elegance

The passion for 'shabby chic' has proved to be more than just a passing fashion whim, and the battered chair, peeling paintwork and faded fabrics still exert their charm. The patinated surfaces and faded colours associated with old furnishings and interiors work well in a non-competitive, non-intrusive environment, which is why pale, muted colours provide the perfect background.

If you have an old property with its own built-in character, a subdued colour scheme will complement the features and allow them to stand out. But faded elegance is not restricted to old houses: it can be created in new or less elegant surroundings with old furniture and furnishings, which will also show up best against light colours. Neither are modern furniture and furnishings incompatible with old and elegant. On the contrary, they can provide a wonderfully fresh contrast against distressed walls and paintwork, well-worn floors and carpets, and can sit happily among other more ornate furniture and decorative items such as mirrors, chandeliers and pictures.

AGEING GRACEFULLY

Furniture

Now that signs of age are a selling point, old furniture has become expensive, but it is quite easy to create an impression of age with simple paint techniques. After painting, imitate signs of wear by rubbing off some of the paint along the edges. For a softer finish, paint furniture with emulsion paint and then give it a sheen with a coat of beeswax, which will also darken the colour slightly.

Floors

Bare wooden floors finished with oil and wax are perfect evidence of faded elegance. If you need a new floor but an old look, buy recycled wood from salvage yards or specialist outlets. Alternatively, paint floorboards with emulsion paint and finish with wax or matt varnish – they will quickly develop their own patina of age. Another option is to apply a limed finish, which gives wood a white-washed appearance. Liming kits are widely available from DIY and decorating stores.

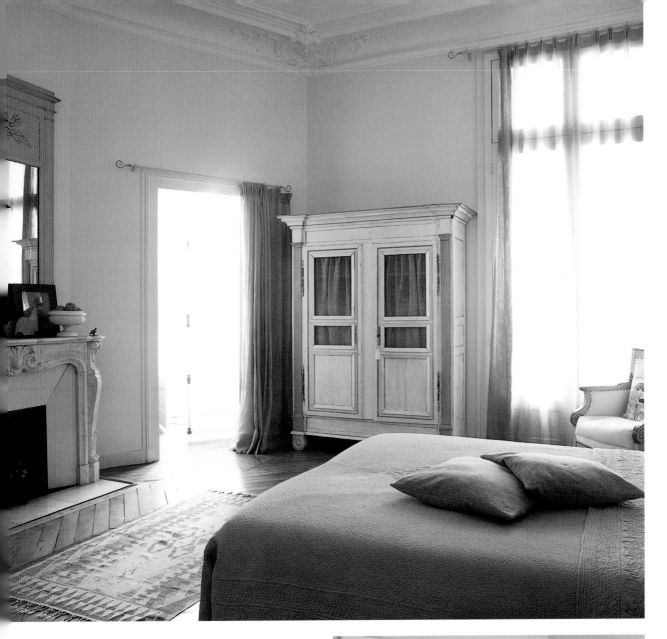

Opposite: *Signs of age such as old paintwork and finishes somehow add elegance and create the impression of a house comfortable in its skin.*

Above: *The neutral palette ensures that nothing disturbs the calm of this room or detracts from the architecture or the antique furniture.*

Right: *A coat of pale paint looks fresh and forms the perfect backdrop here to the scrubbed wooden table and the old paint finishes on the chairs and glass-fronted unit.*

Gentle Tones

Right: *The clean lines of this modern interior are emphasised by the use of harmonising neutral colours and natural materials to create a warm ambience.*

Pale, creamy whites, warm greys and cool beiges are associated with modern, sleek furniture and smooth surfaces, but whereas once the preferred colour for the surroundings would have been white, now you are likely to find other, subtler tones, which soften the atmosphere.

Old white is the new white

Many of the new paint colours, particularly in the historic ranges, are described as white, yet appear not to be white at all. This is because, as we've already seen, it is modern ingredients that make modern paints so white. Old paints were based on lime and chalk, which produced much dirtier colours. These 'old' whites are tinged with varying amounts of green, beige, blue and ochre, which means that some are warm while others are cool.

When these whites were originally developed, they were used in expansive spaces such as large country houses, where they do give an overall impression of white. Now, they provide a chic alternative to pure white and work very well in ultramodern settings. It can be difficult to see from a small sample just how dark or light, warm or cool these colours are. As they can be surprisingly colourful in certain situations, it is a good idea to buy sample pots and try them out before choosing.

Look sharp

If all this relaxation and serenity gets a bit too much, you can sharpen up subtle shades and restrained interiors with smooth, shiny finishes and uncompromisingly contemporary designs. If you feel the need to add refreshing colours, try ice blue and lemon yellow. If you prefer your living and sleeping spaces to be relaxing, confine the wake-up call to kitchens and bathrooms.

SMOOTH FINISHES

● **Gloss paint** – give a gleam to
the pale colours or provide a contrast
with brilliant white paintwork.

● **Glazed wall tiles** – for a change,
use buff tiles in a bathroom: they
give white fittings an extra sparkle.

● **Polished limestone** – use for
walls, sinks, baths, worktops and
surrounds as well as for floors.

● **Ceramic floor tiles** – an
alternative to stone to give your
home a crisp, cutting-edge feel.

MAKE IT WORK FOR YOU

Gentle Tones

There is a wonderful air of serenity in this room that is created by the very restrained, very disciplined colour scheme. Apart from the green walls and touches of gold in the wall-light and chair, everything else is a shade of white, but the overall effect is much richer than would be expected with such a small palette. The combination of the old paint and decorative detailing on the cupboard, plus the the unusual collection of objects on the table, provides a huge number of variations on a theme of off-white, and the gilt on the chairs, wall-light and curtain pole and finial add warm support to the scheme. There is nothing new, or brightly coloured, to disturb this scene, yet despite the fact that all the contents are obviously old, the careful arrangements and use of colour make the room look quite fresh and contemporary. You don't have to have antique furniture or an old property to create this look; it can work just as well with the clean lines of modern furniture and accessories, as long as you restrict the palette to a background colour plus off-white or cream and the mellowing tones of wood.

Opposite: *The furniture and magnificent corals are the centre of attention in this room, which looks calm and uncluttered despite the collections of beautiful objects.*

COLOUR PALETTE

Soft green
This muted green relates to the greeny-tinged gilt on the chair and curtain pole and finial. Although it doesn't impose itself, it provides a dark enough background to allow the furniture and objects to stand out.

Off-white
In this situation, off-white is a loose term used to describe a number of shades that are in many ways indefinable – their subtlety is provided by ageing, texture and nature rather than by pigments.

Gilt
The patina of gilt gives it a warm, greenish tinge, which harmonises with the wall colour and blends in with the general feeling of things that have a past.

Pale khaki
A soft, warm colour – not quite brown and not quite green – this pale khaki will change its appearance depending on the other colours used with it as well as in different lights.

ADDED INGREDIENTS

Furniture
The beautiful cupboard is ornate, yet more rustic than grand, and a plainer, glass-fronted bookcase could work as well. Mixing old and new and different styles makes a more interesting, individual interior. Look for small, unusual chairs in antique markets and junk shops, and rather than a solid upholstered chair, go for an older, more elegant style.

Accessories
Chandeliers and wall-lights give a softer, more romantic light and can be used in a variety of settings, including the very modern. They work best used as a witty addition rather than a centrepiece.

Beautiful objects
The objects in this collection are small in number but big on impact, thanks to their large sizes and wonderful shapes.

Grey Area

Above: *In this bathroom, the grey metallic finishes look crisp and efficient, as well as being a practical choice, and the filing cabinet is a perfect, and useful, addition.*

Opposite:
A roaring fire banishes any coldness associated with concrete, as do the soft, warm grey walls, which also harmonise with the subtle tones of the painting.

Grey is a colour that can look gorgeously sophisticated or desperately dull depending on how it is used. Though pure grey is a mixture of black and white, most versions also contain varying amounts of blue, red, yellow and green to produce a range of colours that can be both striking and subtle. Grey suggests vagueness, and while it could be described as a neutral colour – pale greys are good background colours – it can also be a dominant presence in its darker forms.

Although grey goes with almost any other colour, it also has definite cold and warm identites. Warm versions of grey veer toward pink and sometimes need waking up with a cleaner, sharper colour. Cooler versions contain blue and green, and while their coolness can be asset, especially in a bathroom or kitchen, in other situations, cool greys respond well to the addition of warm or even hot colours.

WARM GREYS

- **Character:** soft, muted, elegant and understated

- **Colours:** mole, elephant, chinchilla, mouse, dove

- **Materials:** velvet, wool, silk, cashmere, grey flannel, carpeting

- **Freshen up with:** white, pale aqua, pale blue, turquoise and chrome yellow

- **Added warmth:** deep pink, burnt orange, deep red, dark brown

COOL GREYS

- **Character:** cool, hard-edged, sharp, functional

- **Colours:** steel, battleship grey, slate grey, granite

- **Materials:** stainless steel, aluminium, galvanised steel, zinc, slate, granite

- **Warm up with:** ochres, oranges, warm reds, deep pink

- **Cool it with:** white, aqua, blue

opalescence

pearlescence

sparkle

seascapes

WATERCOLOUR

silk

TECHNIQUE

glass

reflective

indigo

The transparent and ever-changing nature of water makes it difficult to describe in terms of colour, but it is usually represented in combinations of blues and greens. These variations on a blue/green theme take us from the sparkling brilliance of a Caribbean sea to the almost pea-green tones of a shaded pond, with stormy seas, swimming pools and gently flowing rivers somewhere in between. Water can be stimulating but also soothing, and the same effects can be achieved in interiors. A bright turquoise in the bathroom will wake you up in the morning and soft blues and greens in a bedroom will lull you to sleep at night. Sometimes it is difficult to decide whether a colour is blue or green, and, just as the sea changes colour according to the sky, these water-related colours can change from blue to green depending on the light and the surroundings.

The reflective nature of water suggests colours that are not solid but have depth, qualities that are replicated in reflective surfaces such as tiles. Like water, blues and greens can be made to sparkle, especially when used with shiny metal and glass, which is why they work so well in kitchens and bathrooms. In other situations, the tendency for blues and greens to recede means that they can melt into the background, and for that reason they are also restful colours. However, they also have a reputation for being chilly, and unless used carefully, these colours can be oppressive and dull – though the right shade in the right place can also be surprisingly warm. Many of the pigments used in the creation of blue and green paints and dyes are derived from plants and the earth, and these dry, as opposed to wet, colours have a warmer, more comforting nature, especially when used with other earth colours, or as a foil to some of the more elusive watery tones.

Opposite: The slightly uneven shape, texture and glazed surface of these handmade tiles creates a rippling, watery effect, which makes them a perfect and practical choice for this style of bathroom.

Reflective Mood

In a landscape, the colours associated with water and the sea are difficult to define because any apparent colour is mostly a reflection of the sky. Consequently, the colours are elusive and continually changing according to the light as well as any movement on the surface. The essence of these colours are cool blues and greens and they can be used to create an atmosphere as varied as the landscape itself – often cool and calm but sometimes brighter, more dramatic and stimulating. The watery connections

Opposite: *Mosaic tiles give a more textured and less clinical feel in this generous-sized bathroom. By tiling the walls, storage area, floor and shower screen, the room looks functional yet at the same time luxurious. The collection of baskets are the perfect foil to all the hard edges and surfaces.*

Right: *Who could fail to be energised and invigorated by the intense colour and raw, rustic nature of these Moroccan tiles? Their beauty is enhanced by the fact that they are handmade, which means that no two are the same, and their uneven surfaces give the colour more depth and character.*

make this colour range an obvious choice for bathrooms and kitchens, especially as they are also associated with freshness and cleanliness. It is in these rooms that you are most likely to use glazed ceramic tiles, which as well as being water-resistant, easy-to-clean and functional have a reflective quality, which makes them a perfect medium for water colours. The choice of colour and finish is wide, from the palest aqua to deep aquamarine and even brilliant turquoise, and you can choose the pristine simplicity of plain, smooth finishes or opt for the more characterful variations found in handmade tiles.

As bathrooms are normally small spaces, and used for only short periods of time, they provide an opportunity to try something more daring, expensive or luxurious, and an all-over tiled room can be beautiful as well as functional. In both kitchens and bathrooms, tiles provide an opportunity for a different form of colour, which can either coordinate with the fixtures and fittings or add a splash of colour, such as in a splashback, tiled worksurface or floor.

The reflective surface of glazed tiles will reflect the light and other colours in a room, changing their character and colour depending on how and where they are used. Shiny surfaces respond well to bright illumination necessary for make-up or shaving in a bathroom, or food preparation in a kitchen, but lower levels of lighting can also mellow them and create an atmosphere more suited to relaxing baths or kitchen dining.

The hard surfaces of tiles can make a room feel cold, but you can remedy this by using the warmer greener shades such as eau de Nil and deep turquoise and by using a warmer form of lighting. Wooden floors and accessories will also help take the chill off, as will brightly coloured accessories. For a cool, sophisticated atmosphere, you can also increase the sparkle and freshness with glass, chrome and lots of white.

Right: *Choosing mosaic instead of smooth, evenly glazed tiles gives a warmer and more interesting surface with greater variation and subtlety of colour.*

Restful Mood

Above: *These soft, subdued blue-greens are typical of the colours used on this style of architecture and furniture. Here they add to the feeling of welcome shade from the heat of the sun.*

Opposite: *The gentle colours in these beautiful, rustic tiles are perfectly complemented by the muted tones of the paint on the wall and door.*

Blues and greens based on earth dyes and pigments have a warmth and intensity that makes them restful. These soft, chalky, slightly smokey blues and greens, which are not too dark and not too bright, were much used in old houses, where, accompanied by the mellow tones of old polished wood, they created a tranquil atmosphere.

These are perfect colours for a simply furnished country cottage but also suit grander surroundings, where they look wonderful with red and blue Persian carpets and as a backdrop to ornate gilt-framed pictures and furniture, for example. They also help to create a peaceful ambience in a disciplined modern space and will have a calming influence on livelier, more

colourful and eclectic interiors. These restful colours are widely used in hot climates, where they appear to cool the heat of the sun and blend beautifully with the hotter, earthy colours of the landscape as well as with the traditional architecture, fabrics and artefacts.

Muted blues and greens work best if they are given some air, so keep furnishings to a minimum and clutter at bay. Blinds are preferable to curtains, and, as in hot countries, a restful atmosphere is achieved using lighter forms of furniture such as rattan and wooden-framed chairs and loungers rather than heavy upholstery. Blue becomes grey at night, so in a cooler climate, you may want to add other colours for evening warmth.

PEACEFUL CO-EXISTENCE

A colour scheme made up entirely of blues and greens may be restful, but if monochrome is too monotonous, you may want to enlist other colours to help keep the peace.

● Earth colours

The earthy tones of browns, ochres and burnt orange, whether in the form of wooden furniture and floors or rugs and textiles, will help to counteract any chilly tendencies of blues and greens.

● Reds

Red is often used with blue in rich patterns such as those found in old carpets and rugs, items that add colour and richness without too much contrast to a blue or green environment.

● Pinks

From deep coral to the palest rose, pinks add warmth and a little femininity, if required. Use pinks for cushions and throws in soft textures such as silk, velvet and cashmere, or as rugs and mats in chunky cotton or wool weaves.

● Blues and greens

Lighten the mood with touches of cleaner blues and greens, such as ice blue and pale lime green, in crisp cotton and linen or glazed tiles.

● Black

Furniture and accessories in black laquer, stained wood or metal stand out beautifully against blue, especially if they are ornate items in wrought iron and carved wood.

MAKE IT WORK FOR YOU

Restful Mood

The style of architecture and furnishing suggests that this room
has been designed to offer welcome respite from hot sunny days
and balmy nights. The soft, restful colours and absence of clutter
create an ambience guaranteed to induce a good night's sleep.
Indeed, the overall atmosphere is one of quiet restraint, despite the
ornate furniture and patterned floor. This is because the colours,
typical of this ethnic style, although quite strong, are similar in tone
and are carried throughout, on the walls, paintwork, fabrics, floor
and furniture. The various strengths of blue-green shades are
emphasised by the lighting as well as the matt texture of the walls
and the reflective surface of the tiled floor. The bedcover, table and
paintwork on the door are probably very similar in tone, but the
light and surface textures make them look slightly different.

Not everyone has the luxury of space for a clutter-free bedroom
but if you don't have a convenient alcove for your bed, you could
create a peaceful spot within a busy room by curtaining off the bed,
or a section of the room, using a translucent, coloured muslin.

*Opposite: The
restricted colour
palette, plus plain
walls, sparse
furnishings and
tiled floor bring a
peaceful, cell-like
simplicity to this
bedroom.*

COLOUR PALETTE

Grey blue	Blue	Blue-green	Indigo
This colour works well with other blue-green shades as they are similar to those found in verdigris, which is characterised by variety of tone rather than purity and uniformity of colour.	*A stronger, cleaner blue, which is purer in tone and somehow manages to look warm and cool at the same time. This bright blue will add definition and freshness to a collection of more muted tones.*	*In certain situations, this type of colour definitely looks green, but with different lighting and combined with other colours, it can take on quite a blue appearance.*	*Indigo is a plant dye, which is softer, warmer and more subtle than other, harsher, purer blues. Like denim, this is a colour that looks even better as it ages and fades.*

ADDED INGREDIENTS

Furniture
This ornate style of furniture is easy to find and often inexpensive, but to keep the sense of calm, limit it to one or two pieces. Too many patterned fabrics can look busy: introduce pattern in the form of decorative ironwork on a small table, chair or bedhead instead.

Tiles
For bare floors, tiles are a practical and attractive option. A floor is a good place to add pattern as it won't dominate or distract, especially if colours blend in.

Lighting
These soft colours prefer gentle to harsh lighting. A single source of light positioned above the bed can function as a reading lamp as well as offering general illumination.

Fabrics
Keep things simple with a plain bedcover and limit the pillow count to just two small embroidered cushions. The hanging behind the bed works well as it is delicate and pretty rather than rich and heavy.

Useful Addresses

PAINT AND WALLPAPER

Coley & Son (Wallpapers) Ltd
Ground Floor 10
Chelsea Harbour Design Centre
Lots Road
London SW10 0XE
020 7376 4628
www.Coley-and-son.com
Wallpaper and paint. Traditional and modern designs.

Craig and Rose
Unit 8
Halbeath Industrial Estate
Dunfermline
Fife KY11 7EG
0870 600 1829
www.craigandrose.com
Old established paint manufacturers. Range includes traditional, historical colours.

Dulux
Dulux Customer Care Centre
ICI Paints
Wexham Road
Slough SL2 5DS
09068 515222
www.dulux.co.uk
Large range of products, plus colour mixing service available in large DIY stores and builders' merchants throughout the UK.

Ecos Organic Paints
Unit 34
Heysham Business Park
Middleton Road
Heysham
Lancs LA3 3PP
01524 852371
www.ecospaints.com
Eco-friendly paints, varnishes, woodstains, stainblocks and stone and tile sealants.

Farrow and Ball
Uddens Estate
Wimborne
Dorset BH21 7NL
01202 876141
www.farrow-ball.com
Manufacturers of traditional papers and paints. Widely available in selected DIY stores and decorating shops throughout the UK.

Fired Earth
3 Twyford Mill
Oxford Road
Adderbury
Nr Banbury
Oxfordshire OX17 3SX
www.firedearth.com
Suppliers of paint, wallpaper, wall and floor tiles, bathrooms and kitchens, with showrooms throughout the UK.

Marston & Langinger
192 Ebury Street
London SW1W 8UP
020 7881 5780
www.marston-and-langinger.com
Bespoke conservatories and garden rooms with a range of furniture, accessories and paint.

Morris and Co
Chalfont House
Oxford Road
Denham
Middlesex UB9 4DX
01895 830044
www.william-morris-co.uk
Fabrics and wallpapers based on the designs of William Morris.

Neisha Crosland
Unit 40
Battersea Business Centre
99 Lavender Hill
London SW11 5QL
020 7978 4389
www.neishacrosland.com
Wallpaper and fabrics in distinctive designs.

Paint and Paper Library
5 Elystan Street
London SW3 3NT
020 7823 7755
www.paintlibrary.co.uk
Fabrics and paints. Visit website for stockists throughout the UK.

PAINT, WALLPAPER, FABRICS, FURNITURE AND ACCESSORIES

Cath Kidston
51 Marylebone High Street
London W1U 5HW
020 7935 6555
www.cathkidston.co.uk

Designers Guild
3 Latimer Place
London W10 6QT
020 7893 7400
www.designersguild.com

FABRICS

Colefax and Fowler
110 Fulham Road
London SW3 6HU
020 7244 7427
www.colefax.com
Fabrics and wallpapers. Visit the website for stockists in the UK and throughout the world.

Ian Mankin
109 Regents Park Road
London NW1 8UR
020 7722 0997
www.ianmankin.com
*Traditional cottons and linens
in plains, stripes and checks.*

Osborne and Little
Riverside House
Osiers Road
London SW18 1NH
020 8812 3000
www.osborneandlittle.com
*Fabrics and wallpapers. Visit the
website for stockists in the UK
and throughout the world.*

Sanderson
118-130 Kings Road
Harrogate
North Yorkshire HG1 5HY
01423 568628
www.sandersonfabrics.co.uk
*Suppliers of fabrics, wallpaper
and paint. Visit the website for
stockists in the UK and
throughout the world.*

FLOORING

Crucial Trading
PO Box 10469
Birmingham B46 1WB
01562 743747
www.crucial-trading.com
*Sisal, coir, seagrass, wool and
other natural floor coverings.*

See also:
**The Natural Flooring
Company**
01952 825459
www.thenaturalflooring
company.com

Material Lab
10 Great Titchfield Street
London W1W 8BB
020 7436 8629
www.material-lab.co.uk
*A showroom for the trade and
the public with a wide range of
tiling for walls and floors.*

Sinclair Till Flooring
791-793 Wandsworth Road
London SW8 3JQ
020 7720 0031
www.sinclairtill.co.uk
*Wide range of floor coverings,
including carpets, linoleum,
natural matting, wood, rubber,
cork and vinyl.*

Stone Age
Unit 3
Parsons Green Depot
Parsons Green Lane
London SW6 4HH
020 7834 9090
www.estone.co.uk
*Wide range of stone and tiles
for flooring, walls, worktops,
and basins, as well as for larger
projects such as staircases.*

Stone Theatre
Newnham Terrace
Hercules Road
London SE1 7DR
020 7021 0020

and (showroom):
Ermin Farm
Cricklade Road
Cirencester
Gloucestershire GL& 5PN
01285 869360
www.stonetheatre.com
*Stone flooring and flooring
products.*

UK Wood Floors Limited
34 Invincible Road
Farnborough GU14 7QU
0800 0199 520
www.ukwoodfloors.co.uk
*Solid wood flooring plus
skirtings, doors and furniture.*

Victorian Woodworks
54 River Road
Creekmouth
Barking
Essex IG11 0DW
020 8534 1000
www.victorianwoodworks.co.uk
Reclaimed wood flooring.

FURNITURE, RUGS AND
ACCESSORIES

John Lewis
Oxford Street
London W1A 1EX
020 7629 7711
www.johnlewis.com

Ikea
www.ikea.com
*A valuable source of
inexpensive, well-designed
kitchens, furniture, rugs,
fabrics, bedlinen, kitchen and
bathroom accessories.*

RUGS, RUNNERS AND
KELIMS

Roger Oates
1 Munro Terrace (off Riley Street)
London SW10 0DL
0845 612 0072
www.rogeroates.com
*Contemporary runners, rugs
and fabrics.*

Rugstore
329 Upper Richmond Road West
London SW14 8QR
020 8876 0070
www.rugstore.org
*Lots of old and antique kelims,
rugs, carpets and cushions. Also
cleaning and restoration service.*

MODERN FURNITURE, LIGHTING AND ACCESSORIES

Aram Store
110 Drury Lane
London WC2B 5SG
020 7557 7557
www.aram.co.uk

B & B Italia
250 Brompton Road
London SW3 2AS
020 7591 8111
www.bebitalia.it

The Conran Shop
Michelin House
81 Fulham Road
London SW3 6RD
020 7589 7401
www.conranshop.co.uk

Habitat
08444 991 111 (for branches)
www.habitat.net
*Visit the website for products
and stores throughout the UK.*

Heal's
196 Tottenham Court Road
London W1T 7LQ
020 7730 1234
www.heals.co.uk

SCP
135-139 Curtain Road
London EC2A 3BX
020 7739 1869
www.scp.co.uk

Skandium
86 Marylebone High Street
London W1U 4QS
020 7935 2077
www.skandium.com

Viaduct
1-10 Summer's Street
London EC1R 5BD
020 7278 8456
www.viaduct.co.uk

HOUSEHOLD ACCESSORIES

Baileys
Whitecross Farm
Bridstow
Herefordshire HR9 6JU
01989 561931
www.baileyshomeandgarden.com
*Large range of traditional
household accessories and
hardware for kitchens and
bathrooms, including lighting,
storage and sinks.*

BATHROOM FITTINGS

CP Hart
Newnham Terrace
Hercules Road
London SE1 7DR
020 7902 5219
www.cphart.co.uk
*Bathrooms and fittings from
Europe's leading designers and
manufacturers. Showrooms in
London, Guildford, Esher and
Manchester.*

Ideal Standard
The Bathroom Works
National Avenue
Kingston Upon Hull
HU5 4HS
01482 346461
www.ideal-standard.co.uk

*Large range of modern and
traditional designs, widely
available through large number
of retail outlets and builders'
merchants.*

The Water Monopoly
16-18 Lonsdale Road
London NW6 6RD
020 7624 2636
www.watermonopoly.com
*Range of restored antique
English and French sanitary
ware plus select reproduction
pieces.*

ANTIQUES AND OLD FURNITURE

After Noah
121 Upper Street
London N1 1QP
020 7359 4281
www.afternoah.com

Alfie's Antique Market
13-25 Church Street
London NW8 8DT
020 7723 6066
www.alfiesantiques.com

**The Chandelier and Mirror
Company**
Capel Court Farm
Alders Road
Tonbridge
Kent TN12 6SU
01892 836 820
www.chandeliersandmirrors.co.uk

**Portobello Road Antique
Dealers' Association**
223a Portobello Road
London W11 1LU
020 7229 8354
www.portobelloroad.co.uk
*Visit the website for details of
individual dealers and products
in this famous street.*

ARCHITECTURAL SALVAGE

Lassco
30 Wandsworth Road
London SW8 2LG
020 7394 2100
www.lassco.co.uk

Salvo
www.salvo.co.uk
Visit this website for a directory of registered architectural salvage companies.

TRADITIONAL AND ECOLOGICAL BUILDING AND DECORATING MATERIALS

Francesca's Limewash
34 Battersea Business Centre
99–100 Lavender Hill
London SW11 5QL
020 7228 7694
www.francescaspaint.com

The Green Shop
Cheltenham Road
Bisley
Stroud
Gloucestershire GL6 7BX
01452 770629
www.greenshop.co.uk
Traditional building materials, also technical information and courses.

Mike Wye and Associates
Buckland Filleigh Sawmills
Buckland Filleigh
Beaworthy
Devon EX21 5RN
01409 281644
www.mikewye.com
Lime products, natural building products, paints and waxes. Also repair guide sheets.

Old House Store
Hampstead Farm
Binfield Heath
Nr Henley on Thames
Oxfordshire RG9 4LG
01189 697711
www.oldhousestore.co.uk

DECORATING AND BUILDING ADVICE

The Building Centre
26 Store Street
London WC1E 7BT
020 7692 4000
www.buildingcentre.co.uk
Information, samples and advice on all aspects of products and building materials.

Federation of Master Builders
Gordon Fisher House
14–15 Great James Street
London WC1N 3DP
020 7242 7583
www.fmb.org.uk
A trade association. Use the website to find a local, registered builder.

Polycell Customer Care Centre
ICI Paints
Wexham Road
Slough
Berkshire SL2 5DS
0870 444 1111
www.polycell.co.uk

INFORMATION ON THE CONSERVATION OF OLD PROPERTIES

English Heritage
Customer Services Department
PO Box 569
Swindon SN2 2YP

Tel: 0870 333 1181
www.english-heritage.org.uk

The National Trust
PO Box 39
Warrington WA5 7WD
Tel: 0870 458 4000
www.nationaltrust.org.uk

Society for the Protection of Ancient Buildings
37 Spital Square
London E1 6DY
020 7377 1644
www.spab.org.uk

The Traditional Paint Forum
www.traditionalpaintforum.org.uk
Discussion and promotion of a better understanding and appreciation of traditional paint.

Index